"*Successful living hinges on the capacity to believe. The unconquered and unconquerable of this world are those who have mastered the art of faith. They draw constantly on this inner source of strength, for they have acquired and hold ever fresh in their hearts an abiding* faith in a Higher Power, and in their own destiny."

—*The Authors*

The Art of Real Happiness

(revised edition)

by

Norman Vincent Peale, D.D.

and

Smiley Blanton, M.D.

A FAWCETT CREST BOOK

Fawcett Publications, Inc. Greenwich, Connecticut

THE ART OF REAL HAPPINESS

THIS BOOK CONTAINS THE COMPLETE TEXT OF THE ORIGINAL HARDCOVER EDITION.

A Fawcett Crest Book reprinted by arrangement with Prentice-Hall, Inc.

ISBN   0-449-23039-2

Printed in the United States of America

10   9   8   7   6   5   4   3   2   1

Acknowledgments

THE quotation from Sigmund Freud appearing on page 17 is from his *Collected Papers,* Vol. IV, page 314, and is used by permission of the Hogarth Press Ltd., London.

The selection from *Mind and Body,* by Dr. Flanders Dunbar, on pages 60 and 61, is reprinted by courtesy of Random House, Inc., New York.

Acknowledgment is made to Harper and Row, New York, for permission to include the excerpt from *Grey Eminence,* by Aldous Huxley, on pages 72 and 73.

The poem, "Sleep," appearing on page 73, is from the *Anthology of World Poetry,* edited by Mark Van Doren, and published by Albert and Charles Boni, Inc. of New York.

The poem by Robert Louis Stevenson which appears on page 164, is reprinted from *Poems & Ballads,* and used by permission of the publishers, Charles Scribner's Sons.

The stories of Eddie Rickenbacker, May Ferris, Gene Tunney, Garry Moore and Fred Schwartzwalder and one of the founders of Alcoholics Anonymous were first told in the individuals' own words in *Guideposts,* a magazine published by Guideposts Associates, Inc., at Carmel, New York, and some of them were later reprinted in the book, *Guideposts,* published by Prentice-Hall, Inc., New York.

Contents

The Art of Real Happiness

I   Doorways to a new life for you

Successful living hinges on the capacity to believe. The unconquered and unconquerable of this world are those who have mastered the art of faith. They draw constantly on this inner source of strength, for they have acquired and hold ever fresh in their hearts an abiding faith in a Higher Power, and in their own destiny. Without such faith they are defenseless before the inevitable difficulties that all must face; with it they are armored against even the most cruel of adversaries.

No age has a monopoly on misery, although our own can claim more than its full share, and, at that, misery of a most particular kind. For in the midst of economic plenty we starve spiritually. Surrounded by unmatched potentialities for the good life, we are overwhelmed by the deadly fear that all is lost!

Then the ironic fact emerges that physical medicine, which has triumphed over so many of the bodily diseases that once scourged mankind, has proved utterly inadequate in the treatment of the maladies that canker the modern soul. Hosts of emotional ills gnaw at the roots of our serenity and health, and plague us with shadowy terrors.

But certainly the appearance betrays the reality. Everything is not lost, as one would think! The persistence of such happy affirmations as young people falling in love and, thereby, renewing man's perennial lease on Eden; of teachers unfolding new wonders, and perpetuating old ones, in the minds of youth; of parents nurturing children through unsung years of patience and sacrifice—all of these are the unanswerable rebuttal to the "all is lost" school of thought. All of these and ten thousand other yes-saying acceptances of life reassure us that there is an inexhaustible reservoir from which the human race can draw sustaining strength and hope.

Recently Captain Eddie Rickenbacker, one of the outstanding heroes and leaders of our time, was talking to a group of airmen in a veterans' hospital. The veterans were all men who had been seriously wounded and were, many of them, badly shaken psychologically.

Captain Rickenbacker is a man of inspired and demonstrated faith, and in the midst of his talk he paused, and then said earnestly, "If there is any one of you who has not yet had an experience of God my advice to him is to go out after it and get it." There was a hush in that hospital room. They knew that he had uncovered to them the secret that had brought him through to safety. They realized that this flying ace had pointed out to them the surest way out of their uncertainty and despair.

Rickenbacker does not say such words idly. He does believe that faith is the key to life. "Think positively and masterfully, with confidence and faith," he has said, "and life becomes more secure, more fraught with action, richer in achievement and experience. This is the sure way to win victories over inner defeat. It is the way a humble man meets life or death."

But unfortunately all too many of us have erected barriers in our everyday lives to the healthy operation of belief, to the acquisition of this power-giving faith. A perverse blockage dams the flood of energy that should flow with irresistible force into the healthy heart. What stops this flow? What diverts this stream of hope and belief and confidence that should irrigate the dry and hopeless hearts of men?

These are the questions that are a challenge to every clergyman, to every teacher, to every physician (and especially to every psychiatrist) in our society. Neither are they academic questions. With mounting insistence they enter the lives of troubled human beings who, dangerously close to the breaking point, are unable to live happily in this world until their emotional problems are solved.

In quiet rooms in the Marble Collegiate Church, shut off from the brawling traffic of New York's Fifth Avenue, is a clinic where religion and psychiatry have, we believe, been welded into a powerful therapy for the ills that wrack the human spirit. Here, under the joint direction of a clergyman and a psychiatrist, many harrowed men and women are learning to break down the barriers that keep them from living successfully. Here, day after day, the anxious and the depressed, the worried and the frightened, are gaining the priceless secret of inner peace.

This book is an effort to tell how it is being done.

The clinic of the Marble Collegiate Church was founded over fifteen years ago by a minister and a psychiatrist, the authors of the present book. Each of us, in our own professional work, has long been familiar with the tragedy of those who, with the capacity to stand upright, yet crawled through life on their hands and knees. Despite their wish to move forward joyously, they were tormented with the secret thought, repeated like the ominous ticking of a clock: "I should have done. . . . I ought not to have done." With no place to turn for guidance, no ear to listen to their grief, they naturally became filled with panic and with despair. And for such as these the clinic of the Marble Collegiate Church was established.* It originated our mutual conviction that a new approach was needed to the personal difficulties that beset modern man.

A great adventure for us began! In our minds we dedicated the clinic to a theory, to a dream if you will, that together religion and psychiatry might accomplish more than either could alone. The dream has become a reality; the theory, we believe, a proved fact. The techniques which we have worked out together can, as we believe we have demonstrated time and again, regenerate a person, bring him into touch with his own creative forces and, in turn, with the infinite forces of the universe. This faith-restoring process brings a power and a joy to the individual which he had never dared to hope was possible.

We realized quite early that the people who came to us were a cross section of the troubled millions who, Sisyphus-like, push the cruel stone of anxiety up an endless hill. Most of them had, potentially, the ability to be reasonably content. They were intelligent, well disposed persons who had tried earnestly to follow their best ideals.

* The clinic, now called The American Foundation of Religion and Psychiatry, recently expanded to new offices next door to the Marble Collegiate Church at 3 West 29th Street, New York City.

They were not devoid of religious faith: they prayed; they made use of the sacraments humbly and regularly. But somehow their religion had failed them; it had ceased to be for them a dynamic way of life. In the deepest sense they were cut off from that healthy savor of life, and from a vibrant faith that would give them confidence in themselves and trust in their Creator.

Not only did they lack a sound faith; they lacked self-knowledge. The well established psychiatric fact that the human mind operates on two levels, the conscious and the unconscious, came as a shocking surprise to many of them. The "mind," as they conceived it, was the uniquely human organ that enabled them to remember facts, make decisions, order a dinner, or understand a book. Those and many other functions of the mind were apparently clear to them. But they failed to realize that the conscious part of their minds were merely the uppermost layer of a depthless ocean. They were slow, sometimes unwilling, to accept the fact that most of their mental life was taking place, and most of their behavior was motivated, in these profound depths termed by psychiatry the "unconscious."

The first work of the clinic was to acquaint them with the forces that exist in these depths. Step by step they were shown how conflicts hidden there, particularly those between love and hate, begin in childhood and are often repeated in later life. And it was necessary to explain to them over and over again how these hidden conflicts are reflected on the surface of the mind in the disguised forms of fear, worry, depression, and, significantly enough, a weakening of faith.

It is no accident that loss of faith accompanies other neurotic symptoms. Faith flows from the capacity to love, and this capacity to love may be dulled, or even destroyed entirely, by the bitter struggle between conflicting feelings in the unconscious mind.

An illustration is the story of a young architect who came to the clinic suffering from a profound sense of impending disaster. He lived in the shadow of an unrelenting anxiety. He could not understand it! Its cause did not exist in the outside world; nothing actually threatened him, except his inner sense of dread.

He was the son of a domineering and changeable father, who had persistently frustrated his son's need for love all during his childhood. He recalled one day when his father had promised to spend all Saturday afternoon walking with him in the woods. He was just a little fellow and this had seemed an occasion of great importance. But, when the day came, his father gathered up his golf bag and started off to the country club. When the small boy cried, his father scolded him and called him a crybaby and a nuisance. This episode had been symbolic of all their relationships: one day sympathetic playfulness; the next selfish indifference.

His ability to love anyone or anything was greatly impaired and he carried this impairment of one of the most vital of all human functions into all his later love relationships. By the time he came to the clinic he believed that he had even lost faith in God. "God is a delusion," he said, angrily, during the first interview.

As he gained insight into the true nature of his problem, a burning but hitherto completely repressed and hidden anger toward his father, a powerful mental catharsis took place. The rage that had been poisoning his mind was dissipated. And, after some religious guidance which revitalized his atrophied capacities for love, he not only shook off the painful anxiety which had tormented him since childhood, but he was also enabled to regain his lost faith in God and in mankind.

The first step, then, toward the restoration of faith is to exorcise the devils of submerged emotional conflict. Once the psychiatrist with his specialized skills begins the task of removing these neurotic barriers built of hate, resentment, fear, and anxiety, religious guidance then stimulates an influx of healing faith in the ultimate power and rightness of God.

This, in essence, is the driving force that motivates our entire program at the Marble Collegiate Church clinic.

It may be difficult for some to accept the fact that feelings of which they are completely unaware can distort their lives. Many people actually doubt the existence of these unconscious primitive motivations. They find it difficult to believe that an angelic child, or a mild-mannered man or woman, can harbor the most savage, amoral, and antisocial passions. Since these unconscious impulses are generally exhibited in masked form it is natural to assume that they are not there. And pleasanter! But the evidence of their existence is overwhelming and, *until they are accepted in all their intensity as one of the facts of life, it is impossible to deal realistically with the spiritual anguish which they can cause.*

In his sleep, when the unconscious takes over, man relives in dream form these earliest longings and desires. He re-experiences his old loves, and hates, and fears. During the enigmatic episodes of his dreams, which psychiatry can fully explain only after long study, he expresses the deepest and sometimes the most primitive wishes of his unconscious mind. In these nighttime fantasies he often does not hesitate to love illicitly, or even to kill.

In one of his most celebrated short stories, Robert Louis Stevenson gave the English language a symbol for this basic duality of human nature. But in real life there is no need for a magic elixir such as turned the amiable London physician, Dr. Jekyll, into his primitive counterpart, the bestial Mr. Hyde. To show his teeth, all the average person needs is frustration, sometimes even the most apparently trivial sort. Then suddenly the gunpowder of unconscious rage, stored up in the timeless unconscious, is detonated. The tantrum of the small child, whose scooter is snatched away by an older brother, comes out in the rage of an adult baseball fan screeching at an umpire who has called an obvious ball a strike; or in the disproportionate fury of the housewife berating a maid who has broken her favorite piece of bric-a-brac. But there is, you say, no mayhem here, no actual lusting Mr. Hyde? Of course. As the child represses the murderous content of his rage, so does the frustrated adult. Having learned that society, and his own conscience, demand at least the appearance of self-control, he confines his anger to a burst of temper. He merely blows off steam.

Sometimes these grown-up angers are expressed in very revealing terms. The baseball fan, his eyes popping, screams, "Kill the umpire!" And the housewife, telling her husband about the careless maid, declares casually, "I could have killed her." Such common expressions, not intended literally, actually do reflect the feelings and desires far more accurately than most of us would suspect. Sigmund Freud has described in blunt, and scientifically substantiated terms, the Hyde-like aspects of the average person.

"In our unconscious," Freud wrote, "we daily and hourly deport all who stand in our way, all who have offended or injured us. Indeed, our unconscious will murder even for trifles. And so, if we are to be judge by the wishes of our unconscious, we are, like primitive men, simply a gang of murderers. It is well that these wishes do not possess the potency which was attributed to them by primitive man; in the cross-fire of mutual maledictions mankind would long since have perished, the best and wisest of men and the loveliest and fairest of women with the rest."

We are, of course, morally responsible only for what we think and do consciously. We cannot be held accountable for wishes buried so deeply in our unconscious minds that we are only dimly, if at all, aware of them. But even though we do not translate these wishes into action, they still exist and are able to exert a strong influence on our state of mind.

Psychologically speaking, many people are in an almost constant state of inner warfare without realizing it. Strong, often violent, impulses of a sort absolutely alien to their conscious concept of ethical behavior well up from the "depthless ocean" of the unconscious mind. Their conscious mind rejects them, or represses them as the psychiatrist would say, before they are even fully apprehended. And, through this almost immediate repression, the most painful anxiety arises.

Psychiatry's objective is to enable man to modify and control this primitive side of his nature so that it can be bent to the will, and channeled into useful purposes. It strives to bring a cessation of inner conflict and so restore peace of mind, and to make the reasoning, adult, ethically conscious mind the master of the whole personality.

With methods differing through the centuries, this has been the great task of religion, also. The Church, too often regarded as an institution removed from the main stream of life, is on the contrary a scientific laboratory dedicated to the reshaping of men's daily lives. Its great principles are formulas and techniques designed to meet every human need. The minister, no less than the psychiatrist, is a scientist who works with the human soul. The pulpit behind which the pastor stands is a sacred desk, but it is also a laboratory table on which are performed experiments in the laws of human nature and in the application of spiritual truths.

The New Testament is his textbook of laws: spiritual laws as specific as the laws of physics or chemistry, and compiled by the most subtle and skilled students of behavior. Gathered together in this book the revelation of Jesus Christ is, in simple codified form, a power-releasing mechanism of surpassing therapeutic strength.

As a matter of fact, a re-evaluation of the New Testament in relation to modern psychiatric findings proves it to be beyond question one of the most profoundly astute books on human nature ever written.

Innumerable parallels can be drawn between the fundamentals of the two disciplines. Psychiatry postulates the unconscious, in which it finds not only savage impulses that give rise to fear and anxiety, but also those strivings which are the source of faith, and hope, and of courage, as well as the basis of creative strength. Religion postulates the soul. Charged with evil, this deepest recess of man's being drags him down; but once attuned to God's power, it is the wellspring of his moral strength.

Psychiatry lays bare the innate self-centeredness of the newborn infant. Man, Theology says, is born in sin. And the ethical precepts of religion play an important role in so modifying the child's self-centeredness that he can become a healthy adult, functioning within the social group.

Love and hate are primary concerns of both sciences. Psychiatry says that it is inner conflict, kindled by hatred, which destroys faith. Christianity counters hate with love, instructing that under God all are brothers and that we should love neighbors as ourselves.

Religion and psychiatry alike direct their healing skill toward the release of those inner powers which are possessed by all. The psychiatrist knows that a person can revitalize his whole life once he redirects and alters the character of his disturbing unconscious drives. The concept of change, of spiritual regeneration, is basic to all theory of human behavior. "Do not be satisfied with what you are," the pastor tells his congregation. "Do not give up your dreams of what you may become," says the psychiatrist.

One great scriptural verse which, in many respects, is the very heart of the Christian faith, declares: "If any man be in Christ, he is a new creature: old things are passed away; behold all things are become new." That is to say that if any man fills his mind with Christ's spirit, talks with Him, prays with Him, lives with Him, that man may be completely sure that the old things that have defeated and harassed him shall pass away and all things shall become new.

Modern, dynamic psychiatry has learned that not only can man change through the solution of neurotic conflicts, but that once it is done he can also draw on energies the presence of which he hardly suspected. The clergyman directs himself to the release of man's inner powers: "The Kingdom of God is within you." Through faith in Christ you can attach yourself to the flow of Divine power. "Behold," we read in a great text from St. Luke's Gospel, "I give unto you power to tread on serpents and scorpions, and over all the power of the enemy: and nothing shall by any means hurt you."

It is just such an endless list of parallels between psychiatry and religion that makes the alliance between them so natural and fruitful. At the clinic they are the basis for what we believe is amazingly effective teamwork. Once the psychiatrist has diagnosed the psychic ailment and given his treatment, the minister is enabled to take from the great medicine chest of the Christian faith that remedy best suited for its cure.

The technique of administering the cure is of particular importance. The failure of the Church has often been that it tells persons to pray, but does not tell them how. It encourages them to have faith, but does not give them specific techniques for acquiring it. It tells them to practice love, but gives no detailed methodology for the practice of it in their lives. At the clinic, the important word is HOW.

But before any program for cure can be prescribed, it is necessary to give the person some knowledge of the emotional patterns underlying his behavior. And we encounter some very strange patterns indeed! Perhaps the commonest and most distinctive of these is the feeling of guilt, born of the unconscious desire to injure or kill some other person for wrongs suffered at their hands. This guilt frequently takes the form of an anxiety. It is not uncommon for people to come into the clinic sweating and trembling with a fear the origin of which they do not understand.

Such was the case of a young business man, who complained of a constant sense of fear which was making his life "just plain torture." It made no sense, he told us, but it was there and he could not shake it off. During several interviews it became obvious that his trouble stemmed from a childhood, and lifelong, hatred of his older brother, who had been consistently held up to him as a model. His hatred was so intense that, unconsciously, he wished for his brother's death. This had brought a persistent, overwhelming unconscious fear of being punished.

A staff minister, informed of the exact nature of his problem, was able to show him how to allay his anxiety and regain his faith through prayer. "You must consciously cultivate just ordinary affection for your brother!" he was told. "No matter how hard this may seem, you will have to do it in order to combat the suppressed hatred and anger which has done you so much harm.

"But in order to do that, you will have to change the whole pattern of your thinking. Love, and the faith that flows from it, cannot penetrate your mind while it is suffused and choked by the anxiety you have felt for so long. I am going to give you what I call a prescription to drive out the fear that lies in your mind like a poison. Here is a text from the Scriptures. Take it. Repeat it to yourself over and over again, until your mind is completely possessed with it. Conceive of it as a medicine dropping into your mind, and it will spread a healing influence that will give you an immunity from this fear." As he prayed for this deliverance, he was asked to believe that he received it not at some far off time in the future, but now, immediately!

Inasmuch as the first thing he had to do was get a new spirit in his mind, a spirit of love that would drive out the fear, he was given, as his first text, "Perfect love casteth out fear." He was to use that several times daily for the first week. The second week he was to add another, "I sought the Lord, and He heard me, and delivered me from all my fears."

The next week: "What things soever ye desire, when ye pray, believe that ye receive them, and ye shall have them." The following week: "I will fear no evil: for Thou art with me," to remind him that he was not alone in this fight, but that God was with him, and that God was all-powerful to take away his fears. And still another: "Thou wilt keep him in perfect peace, whose mind is stayed on thee."

This process continued over a considerable period, each week a new text.

He was asked to keep an actual record of how often he repeated each one of the texts the pastor gave him, and he reported later that it was often scores of times in a single day. Gradually, almost like a powerful drug dissipating a center of pain, the religious "prescription" dissolved his fear.

"It's amazing," he told the minister one day. "I've found that those texts are not just words, nor combinations of words! They are power, distilled power."

He was discovering the old truth: that the words of Jesus do indeed have an active healing power; that they are surcharged with light and healing radiance when they are used in a simple forthright way. He found the old truth, also, of the passage in the New Testament, "If ye abide in me, and my words abide in you, ye shall ask what ye will, and it shall be done unto you."

As his anxiety lessened, and his belief in the power of religious faith was gradually restored, a remarkable change came over him. His depressed and beaten look was replaced by one of buoyant self-assurance. Later he told us that his work was very much improved, and that his relationship with his wife and children had become richer and deeper than ever before. A feeling of affection toward his brother, replacing the old antagonism, had laid the groundwork for a new, rewarding friendship. He was, he said, at last finding out what life could really be like.

In the beginning, it was our belief that the association of religion with psychiatry would serve other useful ends beside actual therapy. It has. It has helped to dispel the commonly held notion that psychiatry is in some way unwholesome or connected only with the abnormal side of life. Then, too, many persons earnestly desiring psychiatric help hesitate to seek it for fear of meeting with an attitude of indifference, or even antagonism, to their religious beliefs. Our clinic, of course, solves this dilemma. Here all can be sure of finding psychiatrists who have integrated their medical work with a religious point of view.

We believed it would be a tremendous advantage to have the clinic situated in the church building; and such has been the case. The Church stands for an ancient tradition of love, forgiveness, strength, and protection. In such an environment feelings of guilt tend to be rapidly reduced, which opens the way to a frank discussion of doubts and fears. The church background creates an atmosphere of such trust and confidence that acceptance of the counselor's authority, a vital point in all psychotherapy, is more easily and quickly achieved.

Under these favorable circumstances, recovery from emotional disturbance can often be gained with a rapidity not possible in any other kind of clinic. For example, a woman came to the church in a state of extreme despair. She had a sense of sin so great that it seemed almost to have destroyed her.

This was her story. Five years ago she had become pregnant; a short while later her husband went into the army leaving her alone with her three young children. Financially hard pressed, and emotionally unable to face the responsibility of another child, in her desperation she made the mistake of submitting to an abortion. Although at first in her warped thinking this seemed justified to her, her wrongdoing eventually began to prey on her mind. Regret for her act became an obsession with her. She lost weight, suffered from insomnia and finally began to neglect her children.

Had she prayed for forgiveness? "Yes. I have asked God for forgiveness thousands of times but all my prayers have fallen dead," she answered.

The logic of common sense, which told this woman that her inability to adjust to this past wrong act which she now sincerely repented was abnormal, had no force with her. It was necessary to meet this disability with another technique.

During the conferences it was learned that when she was five years old she had felt a desperate jealousy of a newborn sister, whom she considered to be a dangerous rival for her parents' love. An unconscious wish for her sister's death had stimulated a conscious act and she had tried to injure the baby by jamming a ring down its throat. She was caught in the act and severely punished.

At that moment there was planted in her mind a deep sense of guilt over this wrongdoing which time had neither removed nor even softened. The true significance to her of the abortion in later years could now be understood. The guilt over the desire to be rid of her own child was reenforced in her unconscious mind with the old, infantile wish to destroy her baby sister. And when the old guilt attached itself to the new, her feeling was of such an intensity that no reasoning, nor even the power of prayer and confession, could alleviate it.

Her anguish already somewhat quieted by the confidence instilled by the atmosphere of the church clinic, she was eventually able to accept this explanation. In fact she had an almost immediate sense of release. And when she followed the method of prayer given her, she was finally able to accept the feeling of God's forgiveness that had been denied her for so long. Now, she was able to forgive herself. The change in the woman was amazing. In two months she gained fifteen pounds. She looked much younger and had a joyous contentment which seemed to radiate all about her.

There was one scriptural passage which had proved especially helpful to her: ". . . forgetting those things which are behind," said St. Paul, "and reaching forth unto those things which are before, I press toward the mark." To a person suffering from a sense of guilt, no sounder psychiatric advice can be given.

When we began the clinic, we believed that the fellowship of the church and the value of common worship, a resource not available to the ordinary clinic, would be of great benefit. It has worked out that way. The church is the center of a broad program of social activities; and so when a person comes to us suffering from depression, for example, with a deep need for friendship, and for a real contact with the world, we are able to relate him in a creative way to some group that can fulfill this need. We not only counsel him on his inner problem; we can actually put him in touch with the confidence-inspiring companionship of persons who, like himself, believe in their religious way of life. We can help him integrate his emotional, and spiritual, and social self.

Sometimes this integration is the most important factor in the healing process. We recall a woman who came to the clinic because she felt that her life was empty, without meaning and without hope. A rather pathetic person, with a listless manner and an extraordinarily drab and untidy appearance, she said that she was on the edge of a "nervous breakdown."

Two facts about her eventually came out which, to the untrained eye, might have seemed unconnected but which actually gave the clue to her basic problem. First: some years before, her father, a querulous, complaining man, had retired and come to live with her, and ever since then she had waited on this demanding slave-driver hand and foot, to the point where there was no time in her life for even the slightest sort of relaxation. She maintained a conscious attitude of almost morbid dedication to the unrewarding task of caring for him. And she had resigned herself, as well, to the necessity of becoming a frustrated old maid.

Questioned, she said yes, of course she loved her father, even though he was difficult and cranky. She obeyed the bibilical injuction, "Honor thy father and thy mother." At least she had convinced herself that she did. Actually, though, as she was eventually able to see, she had only succeeded in bottling up a seething anger at her father because he was limiting her life so cruelly. She had done so complete a job of this that she was absolutely unaware of her real attitude toward him.

The second pertinent fact revealed was that at the place where she worked she was continually having accidents. As we have said, it is a common trick of the mind to drive back into its unconscious depths ideas and feelings which are repugnant or frightening. In her unconscious mind, however, the suppressed rage had aroused an appalling sense of guilt. The guilt, in turn, had taken the not unusual form of self-punishment.

"Self-punishment?" She looked puzzled.

"Of course," the counselor told her. "Don't you see? Those accidents you have been having really are self-inflicted punishment for your hostile feelings toward your father."

Insight into the true nature of her buried emotions was half the battle. With understanding of it, her hostility and the accompanying guilt began to melt away. She was then able to develop a more normal attitude toward her father, to say a firm but loving "no" to his excessive demands on her. Her anxiety lessened and the accidents eventually stopped altogether.

Meantime she was advised to give some well considered attention to her appearance, her clothes, and her hair, and to learn the art of judicious make-up. It was arranged to get her launched in the social life of the church. And subsequently she met a suitable young man, fell in love, and was engaged to be married. In brief, every aspect of her life was changed.

The technique which has been developed at the clinic varies only in detail; the broad principles are by now well established. The staff has necessarily grown until now it includes seven consultants. The first interview may be with either a minister or a psychiatrist, more or less by chance. The main course of the therapy may be directed more or less equally by both, or almost entirely by either one, all depending on the exact nature of the problem. Sometimes a single interview is sufficient; more often several are required; occasionally a great many.

There is no claim made, of course, that every troubled person can be basically affected by this combined therapy. Some mental and emotional disturbances are so deep-seated that they can be remedied only by the most prolonged psychiatric treatment. Others are such that they yield quite rapidly to religious guidance alone. But in countless cases of persons who worry and fret and feel inadequate to the fulfillment of their desires, the alliance between the two disciplines has a marvelous effectiveness.

The child, said Wordsworth, is father to the man. And for many persons, reeling under the shock of life in this age, this parentage is their undoing; for the shackles of unresolved conflicts placed upon them in childhood remain to enslave them in their adult life. Our hopeful message is that a way is at hand to help remove these fetters. They can, we believe, be most effectively struck off by the combined blows of modern dynamic religion, and of psychiatry.

In succeeding chapters we shall try to tell the whole story of what is being accomplished; of how the principles and methods that are worked out in the clinic can be of direct benefit. Perhaps in these pages you may find the answer to your problem or to the problems of those dear to you. The ministers and the psychiatrists of our clinic, joined in a common love of people, unitedly assert to all who sense failure in their lives that it is never too late to find through faith the sources of power which give man courage; never too late to acquire faith in one's self, in other people, other causes, and other ideals; and, above all, never too late to find a creative faith in God.

II *Why do we love and hate at the same time?*

A young mother, bewitched by the soft warmth of the first day of spring, takes her six-year-old child for an afternoon expedition to the zoo. At the start all is light-hearted joy and happiness. They walk hand in hand in the delightful sunlight. Then the little boy, suddenly slipping away from her, becomes lost in the crowd. After half an hour of agonized search she finds him, not, as she had dreaded, fallen into the bear pit, but ecstatically watching the sea lions. Her first relief switched to anger, she slaps him. His bliss is at once transformed into furious resentment; he bursts into tears.

Repentant, she buys the child an ice-cream cone and his resentment is magically changed to pleasure. Once more they love each other. But then he wants another cone. She refuses, it would spoil his supper. He dissolves into shrieks of rage. Once more they are angry. After half a dozen or so such episodes, worn out by their extremes of love and anger, they take the bus home, his sleepy head resting trustfully on her shoulder. All is love again.

How often do the daily lives of married couples, their quarrels and disagreements translated into adult terms, follow a roughly comparable pattern?

The mother and child, brother and sister, wife and husband, and countless bickering friends love each other. Of course they do. But the generally unpalatable truth is that they hate each other also. Love is almost never undiluted; it is nearly always mixed with some portion of hatred, resentment, or dislike.

These two states do not necessarily alternate. A curious fact has emerged from psychiatric investigation: that we have the capacity for almost simultaneously loving and hating the same person. Psychologically this can create havoc. A constant, exaggerated oscillation between love and hate, characteristic of those who have not learned the mastery of these two powerful emotions, becomes a sadly wearing, exhausting business.

The psychiatrist views love and hate in a somewhat special way. His definition of love comprises all feelings of attraction, at every level of intensity, from the passionate attachment between young lovers to the simple affection of friend for friend. Within his broad category of hate are included all feelings of repulsion, from blind fury down to the mildest resentment or dislike. Like the positive and negative charges of electricity that hold together the whirling electrons and protons of the atom, love and hate, in the psychiatrist's view, are the positive and negative forces that determine men's relationships with each other.

This dynamic concept of love and hate, dimly felt always by philosophers but forged and perfected in a half century of intensive research, is a touchstone of the psychiatrist's healing art. The physicist, having penetrated the secret of the atom, can unleash its gigantic force. The psychiatrist, having discovered this particular law of man's inner being, can help him to tap his vast potential emotional energies. And in this task, as our experience at the Marble Collegiate Church clinic has, we feel, repeatedly proved, the dynamic ministrations of religion are a unique and invaluable ally.

Not only the atom, but all of nature, exhibits a duality, a flow of power between opposites. The tides rise and fall. Surf beats upon the long shore, recedes, and rushes in again. The heat of summer gives way to winter cold. Night follows day.

There is a duality, too, in the inconstancy of people's moods, reflected in their ceaselessly shifting attitudes toward each other. And when we examine this inconstancy with the so-called depth analysis of psychiatry, we find at its core a changing current of love and hate rising from the bottom of the unconscious. It is only as we become masters of the duality inherent in our natures, and achieve a healthy balance between our love and hate, that we are able to achieve inner peace. But if we are mastered by it, twisted by the excesses of our emotions whose origin we have never fully comprehended, we are the unhappy victims of incessant unresolved conflicts.

Love ... hate ... love ... hate ... love ... hate ... hate and love, they follow each other across the pages of some lives in a ceaseless, often bewildering, and seemingly irrational succession.

We love what gives us pleasure, hate what gives us pain; we love what fulfills our needs, hate what frustrates them. This is natural enough. But there are people so surcharged with unconscious resentment, that life for them is an almost constant procession of minor or major annoyances. Like trigger-happy soldiers firing at leaves rustling in the dark, they let fly their anger at the merest shadow of frustration. And when they meet real setbacks it is with a rage of truly staggering intensity. Such persons almost daily sacrifice their peace of mind to the destructive, corroding passion of their hatreds.

Let us illustrate this point. An artist had sold a picture and he decided to invest the proceeds in the stock market. He telephoned an old and trusted friend, a broker, to ask for his advice. He wanted some action for his money, he insisted, a stock that would increase in value rapidly. The friend, after rather extensive warnings that all such operations involve risk, reluctantly suggested a speculative type of security.

At this point the artist brimmed with love for his old friend. He saw in him an all-wise, kindly benefactor who had opened the way to sudden riches. His fertile imagination, spurred on by the most grandiose wishful thinking, gave the shares of stock a veritable dream value. This, unhappily, they never actually attained. A minor market crash, as a matter of fact, reduced their value within a few days to less than half of what he had paid for them.

What happened then? The friend, who still possessed all the qualities the artist had once loved, now suddenly became the target of his venomous hate. The artist never stopped to remember the warnings, or to take at least some of the blame for his misfortune. No, he could only see his shattered fantasy of easy money and he compulsively put all of the responsibility for it on his friend.

True, it is not pleasant to lose hard-earned money. But he was only compounding his misery by an unreasoning hatred so intense and out of all proportion that it brought him to our clinic door soul-sick with anxiety.

Most often, and particularly when they are aimed at someone bound to us by family ties, our deepest hates are repressed, banished to the unconscious mind. By a sort of law of self-protection, we permit ourselves to be consciously aware in general of only the loving side of our emotions. We refuse to see the true character and depth of the hate that lies beneath our angers and irritations. The disturbing, frightening idea of hatred toward a loved one is simply too much to tolerate. But repression does not make it disappear, nor even hide it.

Unconscious hate is like a specter haunting us from the shadowy places of our lives; and sometimes in our dreams we get a frightening glimpse of it. For example, a woman in her early fifties—we will call her Mrs. J.—was brought to our clinic as an emergency case. Her daughter, who accompanied her, was justifiably alarmed by her mother's pitiful state of shaking, trembling panic. It was some time before Mrs. J. could pull herself together sufficiently even to admit to the psychiatrist in the clinic that she was desperately frightened. Her heart was palpitating. It was so hard for her to breathe that she was nearly suffocated. She actually felt as though she were going to die.

"It began last night," she said in a gasping voice. "I woke up suddenly, absolutely terrified. Then I remembered that I'd had a horrible dream, a nightmare of some sort. But I couldn't recall what it was about. I still can't. I just felt that something terrible was going to happen, and that feeling has been getting worse ever since."

In the quiet atmosphere of the clinic consultation room she slowly became calm enough to give a brief account of her life, from which the counselor gathered these key facts. She had four children, all grown and happily married. Her husband, a somewhat irascible, quick-tempered man, was a strict disciplinarian toward his whole family, including her. Although he was what is called a "good provider" he was rather close with his money, often accusing her unjustly of extravagance, of careless management of the household affairs, and she found this very disturbing.

She respected and loved her husband. But, she admitted, he had kept her from doing many things she would like to have done. To illustrate, she had been interested in painting and etching when she was a girl and had recently thought seriously of taking it up again. But her husband had quite callously made fun of this, saying it was ridiculous for a woman of her age to fool around with such childish interests.

Of recent years, her husband was away on business trips a great deal of the time. When he was at home he was generally worn out by his professional activities, which encompassed his whole world, and would spend the evening reading the paper until he went to bed. There had been less and less companionship between them.

In short, Mrs. J. was frustrated by her life, emotionally starved, with no satisfactory outlet for the creative, loving side of her personality.

"You know," the psychiatrist said to her, "very often a dream such as the one you had last night is stimulated by something that occurs during the day. Tell me, did anything unusual happen yesterday?"

Rather hesitantly she said, "Why, yes. You see, about two weeks ago my husband had an attack of coronary thrombosis while he was in Chicago on a business trip. Then, yesterday, I had a letter from his doctor saying he was out of danger and well enough to come home soon."

Then the counselor suggested to her that clearly, since there was nothing in the outside, objective world to cause her anxiety, there must be some other explanation; some profound emotion that had been stirred up in her unconscious mind by the letter, and so precipitated her acute state of fear. What they must do now was to try to find out what subjective factor had aroused her alarm. In the meantime, he suggested, a clinic pastor would help her to get some immediate release from her anxiety.

The pastor, receiving Mrs. J. in a pleasant, book-lined room more like a library than a clinic, had her sit in a chair in which she could lean back comfortably. He explained to her something of the workings of the deeper part of her mind in which, he told her, much of our spiritual life takes place. "If you can delve into that inner, creative side of your nature now," he said, "your immediate fear can be dissipated and you can feel at ease while we are finding out more about what is troubling you. I want you to relax, close your eyes, and repeat after me the following prayer:

"Oh Lord, help me to understand the deeper recesses of my mind and to know that God dwells there in me. Help me to come in contact with the inner strength which he places there, that I may have peace of mind."

The minister then asked her to repeat after him several

phrases from the Scriptures and from old hymns, to conceive of them as dropping softly into the very depths of her unconscious mind. She was to say them slowly, thoughtfully, savoring their exquisite melody and healing power: "I will fear no evil: for Thou art with me." Again: "Jesus, Lover of my soul, let me to Thy bosom fly." And another: "Rock of Ages, cleft for me, let me hide myself in Thee."

He then sat with her for several minutes during which he asked her to be silent and think of the love of God. She was to meditate upon God's peace, and conceive of the cool, healing quietness of His touch as resting upon her heart and mind.

"Now," the minister said, "I feel quite certain that your fear state is considerably reduced. In fact, it is eliminated, and you can go home with calm in your mind. The three of us, the psychiatrist and you and I, are going to work out your problem."

Eventually, after several further interviews with the pastor and the psychiatrist, Mrs. J. was able to face the critically important fact that her husband, by frustrating nearly all of her desires for outgoing, constructive activities, had aroused in her a resentment so strong that she had unconsciously wished he might die instead of recover and so set her free. The doctor's letter about his health had undoubtedly stimulated this death wish to such an extent that it broke toward the surface of her mind in the nightmare she had mentioned. This had been the immediate cause of her anxiety. We were sure, and time proved us right, that her insight, together with religious guidance and the resulting recrudescence of faith, would permanently relieve her of her fears and make it possible for her to be more tolerant toward her husband.

But she still had an objective difficulty. It seemed unlikely that her husband would basically change his attitude toward her; furthermore, being the sort of man he was, if his heart proved to be seriously affected he would undoubtedly push himself into chronic invalidism.

The next step for her was to organize her life so that no matter what happened she could express her long starved creative feelings. She finally decided to go to an art school, to take up painting in a serious way. We have since heard from her that she did this, and that she was having a modest professional success. But, more important, her new avocation brought her a steady source of happiness and escape.

Mrs. J's story is an excellent illustration of how religion and psychiatry combine so effectively in attacking psychic ills. Ordinarily a person suffering from so profound a hatred might require months, even years, of patient therapy by psychiatry alone. But the feeling of confidence inspired by the understanding protective guidance of the minister, joined harmoniously with real insight, frequently compresses the whole process into a few weeks or months to a point, at least, where the person can resume living.

People have the capacity for almost simultaneously hating everyone they love. This peculiar love-hate pattern is formed in infancy and childhood.

In earliest infancy a person exists, as he never will again, in a most delightful state of continuous self-gratification. Spongelike he absorbs endless amounts of food, warmth and fondling. This is pure rapture. But it is too good to last. He begins, very gradually, to sense the presence of an intruder, generally his mother, in his tiny paradise. At first he had accepted her as hardly more than an extension of his own body, as a sort of magic cornucopia from which he could draw inexhaustible bodily pleasures. Then it dawns on him that she is another, a separate person.

And, furthermore, this intruder has a will of her own that may, and does, collide with his tyrannical wishes. Grudgingly, in return for value received, he yields to his mother a small share of the love which until now he has devoted entirely to himself. But he charges a small price for it in the form of resentment toward her at making him give up even the tiniest part of his self-love, in adjusting himself to her wishes.

It is a faint enough emotion, this tiny resentment, but it is the spark that will kindle into the first flame of his hate.

Because for a time his every desire was immediately

satisfied, the infant develops delusions of grandeur on a minute scale. He fondly believes that merely to wish for something is to have the wish automatically granted. This becomes a delusion and a snare. As he leaves his crib for widening exploration of the house, then the yard outside it, many of his wishes have necessarily to be balked.

He does not take kindly to his increasing conflict with the restrictions of the outer world. A child wants what he wants when he wants it, and in a rather violent way. Give a three-year-old his supper when he is hungry and he gurgles with delight; try to make him eat it when he is not and he is likely to direct toward you an anger of such malevolence that if he had a machine gun he would behave like a criminal. Actually, though, because he depends for his very life on his parents, he immediately represses most of his hostility into his unconscious mind. He tries, but he is not always completely able, to keep from expressing it.

A young mother tells of sitting before the fireplace with her five-year-old boy while she entertained him with a bedtime story. When he picked up a poker and began punching at the logs, she said, "Tom, when you do that you knock the logs down and make smoke come into the room." He continued, and then she took the poker away from him. He was silent for a moment, then turned to her and said vindictively, "I'm going to cut *you* up and throw *you* into the fire."

The fact is that through a long series of frustrations, many of them inevitable and necessary, a child's capacity for resentment first ripens into strong dislike, then hate, to a point where he becomes quite capable of death wishes toward those he loves most. This is a critical period in every person's life. For at this precise time his love-hate pattern is being set and, under certain circumstances, it may be a grievously crippling one throughout all his years.

If a child's frustrations are kept at a minimum, if he is given a perfectly balanced love, his hatreds too are minimized. They are largely absorbed by his love. But to determine such perfect balance is almost as thorny a problem as the medieval one of how many angels could dance on the point of a needle! And, in truth, most parents, being human, lack the perfect wisdom and fortitude required by the task.

What is most apt to happen is that children are hemmed in by a maddening barrage of "do's" and "don't's," and are given either too little or, equally frustrating, too much love. The result is that their fierce resentments are not off set by their more powerful love. On the contrary, neurotic hate piles up in their timeless unconscious minds in which every thought and feeling glows as brightly ten or fifty years later as the day it first occurred. In later life these pent-up, deathless hatreds continually erupt in the most bewildering and distressing forms.

Such was the case of a lawyer, and a successful one, who brought to our clinic the complaint which, in the past ten years, we have most frequently encountered—depression. No day in his life began, he told us, without a tormenting sense of depression of the blackest, most threatening sort. And yet there was not one single objective fact in his life, as far as he had been able to figure out, which justified it. There was only one way in which he could find the answer to this baffling paradox.

Know thyself is a dictum as old as philosophic thought. "Do not weep," Spinoza said, "do not wax indignant. Understand." But the truth was that this young lawyer, without skilled help, could no more understand the real dynamics of his mind than a child, gazing at a winter sky, could divine the logic of the stars. And so a psychiatric counselor had to direct his searching down the path of self-exploration.

The lawyer's father had been in his day one of Broadway's top actors. A temperamental, volatile man, his attitudes toward his son had blown hot or blown cold, but were always unpredictable. Naturally, they had never got on well together and now, although they were adults, they quarreled whenever they saw each other.

He recalled an incident which took place when he was six years old. His father was expected home after an absence of several months of nation-wide touring with a road company. The boy, longing to see him, waited for him in the front yard. But, when he rushed eagerly toward his father, ready to spring into his arms, he was abruptly brushed aside. His father was tired and moody. All that he can remember now was that at that moment he felt utterly crushed; for him the end of the world had come.

To the casual eye this was a simple incident, a childhood upset, perhaps sad, but of no great consequence. The psychiatrist knew better. In the light of many additional facts slowly uncovered, it became obvious that this incident had crystallized into a deadly pattern in the boy's life. He craved his father's love. He needed it. Reacting to this single gesture of rejection, which was symbolic of all the many past frustrations and denials, all of his suppressed rage exploded. His hatred flashed out like lightning; but, ironically enough, its target was the boy himself, not the father.

A child's wild anger at a parent can be a damaging experience. And even consciously he expects dire reprisals for his savage feelings. In his tortured imagination, he envisages a punishment tailored to the dimensions of his rage.

It was clear that this lawyer had repressed the knowledge of most of this hostility. But in his unconscious mind the old childish hate, penned in by a devastating fear of punishment, continually stirred up a lifelong resentment toward his father, and still smoldered hotly within him. Such neurotic hate narrows the flow of all love down to a trickle. His normal affections were so dammed up that he could not properly love himself, nor those around him, nor, although he was an active church member, his Creator. Small wonder he was depressed!

The pastor recommended to him that he make a persistent conscious effort to alter his own attitude toward his father. He asked him to try to see that his father had probably done the best he could within the limitations of his own unstable temperament. Then the pastor gave him a method of prayer to follow which, when added to a better understanding of his own inner feelings, proved to have a marvelous effectiveness. He was asked to repeat aloud several times each day these affirmations of faith:

Through God's goodness, there is nothing wrong with me except my wrong thinking, which is now being corrected.

God is now filling my body, mind and soul with courage and strength.

I completely surrender myself to God and trust Him and have faith in His loving kindness. I know he forgives me for my old feelings of resentment and hate. This forgiveness is happening now.

God will give me strength to achieve a full, satisfying life, which I now believe is possible.

In the course of time, as his depression faded, what he asked for in his prayer was, happily, granted to him.

To grasp more fully how emotional patterns formed in infancy and childhood can effect so decisively all later relationships, we must discuss one of the most fascinating patterns of the mind. It is called "transference." For our purposes here, transference may be defined as the act of ascribing to other people the characteristics of those with whom we are associated in our earliest years. And it follows that our attitudes toward them, our loves and hates, trace, if uncorrected, something of the same pattern. It is through transference that we are able to make those emotional relationships with others which are necessary to us as social beings. A child's emotional life widens constantly as he comes in contact with the world of people. And those emotions which he transfers to them from his earlier relationships are shaped in the mold of this earlier love and hate for his own parents.

It is primarily through this same process that a child arrives at his first concept of the Supreme Being. For when he realizes that his earthly father is not the omnipotent creature he once fondly imagined, but has human weaknesses and deficiencies, he does not abandon his quest for such a figure. He simply transfers his yearnings and devotion to a truly perfect, all-powerful image, the image of God. This is the beginning of the religious life.

The transference of our emotions from our parents to other persons and to the Creator is a normal and enriching activity. But, unfortunately, it can go astray. For, since the earliest love-hate feelings toward our parents are the prototypes of all our later expressions of emotion, if these feelings were, in childhood, distorted by frustrations, the transference of love and hate in adult life will follow a painful, trouble-making course.

A person whose mind is loaded with explosive resentment is hardly capable of serene, fruitful relationships with anyone for he creates his world in the image of his early disturbing family situation. To him God appears as punishing and tyrannical. Through a distorted form of transference he compulsively makes employers, friends, and others into symbols of mother, father, brother, or sister. Then, having endowed them in this way with fantasied qualities that they do not actually possess, he directs his neurotic hate toward them in accordance with the old design.

The records of our clinic are filled with the stories of persons who have built for themselves this all too common kind of psychological trap. Let us briefly examine four such cases.

A man with considerable executive ability had felt compelled to move to five different firms in the past eleven years. We discovered that in every instance his behavior had followed the same peculiarly rigid pattern. He invariably endowed his superior with superhuman qualities of kindliness and justice. Without realizing it, what he actually did was to regard his employer as being a kind of father that he had always wanted but had never had. This man's exaggerated expectations of a father's loving treatment could hardly be fulfilled by any employer. But that was what, unconsciously, he demanded, and as a result he continually suffered from bitter disappointment.

On his last job he complained to his superior, a company vice-president, that his contractual agreement was not being observed. When the vice-president asked to take the contract home with him to study it, the man naïvely handed it over to him, even though he had been repeatedly warned that this hard-boiled employer was given to sharp practices. The next day he found out that the vice-president had calmly torn up his contract. There was nothing to be done about it. And this disaster, climaxing a long series of failures, reduced him to a state of the most pitiful confusion and anxiety.

The second was a boy who came to our clinic seriously troubled because he had twice run away from college and was now afraid to return. He was intelligent, able to pass examinations easily, but he simply could not stand the discipline of classwork. He admitted having expressed such antagonism toward his professors that he was constantly in hot water.

Many persons automatically react negatively to anyone in authority. But what was wrong here? The boy's mother died when he was four years old. He had been brought up by his father and a stepmother. And, as it happened, his father was an exacting, irritable man who unrelentingly criticized him from morning until night: his table manners, his appearance, his friends, his speech, his ideas, indeed, everything about him. So, later on, making all figures of authority, including his professors, into images of his harsh father, he unloosed on them the fury he had been too frightened to heap upon his real father. This was so painful to him at college, that he could not bear it. And so he ran away.

The third was a brilliant young chemist who had worked out an improved formula for a new plastic and went into business with a partner who was to handle the sales. Things went smoothly for a while; then, although he was unable to be specific about it, he began to feel that his partner was not devoting enough time to the business. He became so upset about this matter that he went to a lawyer to make arrangements to have the partnership dissolved.

As we finally proved to him, he was acting on the basis of infantile impulses, not reality. And this is why he did it. This young man, whose childhood had been marked by very severe frustration, tried to compensate for it by an overly close relationship with his brother, to whom he devoted an abnormal amount of love. Then the brother had died. Ever since that he had tried to make others, among them his partner, take his brother's place. This no man could do. And when the partner failed to treat him as a loving brother, but naturally enough, as a business associate, he felt furiously disappointed. His anger and resentment, unjustified as they were, made him sick in mind and heart.

The fourth is a business man who suddenly fell into a panic accompanied by headaches so severe that he was hardly able to work or sleep. During his first interview at our clinic he happened to mention the fact, which had caused him much annoyance, that his secretaries would never stay with him for more than a few months. Indeed his last secretary, after refusing to handle several personal duties for him, including arranging for his laundry and shopping for his shirts and ties, "gave him a piece of her mind" and left. This was when the panic and the headaches started.

He was unmarried. He had lived with his mother, who had smothered him with love from infancy, and on whom he had an unhealthy dependence, until he was thirty-five. As we have said, too much love from a parent can be as disastrous as too little. Since her death a few years previously, which was a terrible blow, he had unconsciously tried to make other women act toward him as tender mothers. He had failed to appreciate the unique quality of each mother, which is that no one can replace her. Yet he persisted in this, particularly with his secretaries, and when he met with a rather violent refusal to take over a mother role, his flaring resentment made him ill.

The cause of these trouble-making transferences is deep-seated; the cure is far from easy. But, as we have proved time and again at our clinic, intellectual insight goes a long way. Self-knowledge, a true understanding of when and how love and hate became so cruelly intertwined in one's self, is the first step. It is essential for these perplexed, unhappy persons to see quite clearly and specifically that they themselves are the cause of their disturbing resentments, dislikes and hatred, and not those toward whom they are directed.

A vital part of the therapy lies in changing their attitudes as completely as possible; of even making an effort to transform hatred toward a person whom they have bitterly resented into a positive love. This is never easy, but sometimes it can be done.

Above all they must be shown the satisfying wisdom of no longer directing their natural craving for a perfect friend toward imperfect human beings, but toward the only Being who can measure up to such standards, to all-perfect God. The pastors in our clinic complete the healing, in such cases, by helping the patients to establish a normal and satisfying relationship with God. They are stimulated to follow an ancient precept: "Render ... unto Caesar the things which are Caesar's; and unto God the things that are God's." The price that a person pays for failing in the proper management of his love and hate is a very heavy one. He typically vacillates between unwarranted hopefulness and black despair. Minor irritations frustrate him beyond all reason; he is like to magnify the smallest adverse incident into a gross affront. He can hardly ever sustain stable, satisfying relationships with anyone. He feels alone and deserted, by God and by man.

On the other hand, the rewards for mastering this subtle art of self-management are great. A man who has done so feels sustained by faith in a protective, benevolent deity. He is hard to frustrate. Not easily giving way to irritation or despair, nor easily transported to heights of unreal ecstasy, he pursues a reasonably even pace. Viewing the foibles of others, and his own, with a certain tolerance, he expects neither the best nor the worst to happen, but is fortified by a reasoned optimism. For him a certain amount of necessary aggressiveness is the salt which makes the feast of life more savory. He reserves his real hatreds for those things which deserve it: real, not imagined, injustices, such as cruelty and bigotry.

Not forever suspiciously questioning the motives and acts of those around him, he can give his love generously and wisely and receive a generous measure of love in return. And he has a genuine faith that if he does his best things will work out for him, at least within the limits of this uncertain and far from perfect world. When the blows of unavoidable hardships or disappointments strike, he does not struggle wildly and inflexibly against them but, like a seasoned fighter, learns to roll with the punch.

Such, briefly, is a person who, having learned to manage his love and hate, is able to accept reality. He views the world and his fellow men as they really are, not as his infantile neurotic wishes tell him they ought to be.

There is, of course, no easy way to accomplish this balanced, happy way of life. But, from our long experience, we offer these few simple rules:

1. Accept the idea that some feelings of strong resentment toward loved ones are not shocking, or immoral, and are not unnatural. You can only rid yourself of them by self-knowledge, never by denying them.

2. Be sure that your feelings toward people are justified by actual circumstances. For example, do not hate a person because he resembles someone who wronged you. Do not endow a person with truth and kindness because he resembles someone you love.

3. Try to deal objectively with people, according to what they really are. Do not make a friend into a brother; a wife or secretary into a mother; a husband or employer into a father.

4. Do not ask a person to be what he, or she, is not. Do not ask or expect from a person what he cannot give.

5. Give your loved ones the love that is their due. Reserve your higher love for God, realizing that He is the only unchanging, never-failing support in which you can rest utter confidence.

6. Take for your motto: "If God be for us, who can be against us?" and you will find yourself possessed of a dignity and strength which will make you equal to any occasion.

No one can avoid entirely an inner struggle between love and hate. We are all challenged by it. The question in everyone's life is not whether his feeling of hate and aggression can be done away with, but whether it can be successfully modified. We believe that love can control hate. It is our conviction that through the insights and teachings of today's religion and psychiatry, men and women can win such victories in their own personal lives. In this way they can gain a firm foothold on the path of inner peace.

III   *How you can have peace of mind*

Recently the sales director of an importing firm came to us for help because, as he put it, he was worried sick about himself. He had lost all self-respect. He was convinced that he had become a thief. His reasons for thinking so were most curious. He accused himself of stealing money from his company by falsifying his expense account.

On being questioned, he had to admit that there had been no complaints by his firm. The clinic adviser then went over his expense sheets with him and found what we suspected, that, if anything, he had been cheating himself in his attempts to avoid dishonesty. You might think that this would have brought him a great sense of relief. But no logic could satisfy this man that this was really the case: the idea that he was stealing had become an unshakable and tormenting obsession.

The clue to this puzzle in human behavior was revealed only after many long and patient interviews. About ten years previously this man had been unfaithful to his wife. At the time he told himself that no one would ever know, and he managed to justify it in some way, and forget about it.

Or so he thought. But it became clear to the psychiatrist that his present feelings of guilt really stemmed from that incident, even though it had happened so long ago. But for some reason, in his unconscious mind, he preferred to regard himself as dishonest about money rather than as having committed an infidelity, and he had transferred his lingering sense of guilt about his extramarital relations to the way in which he handled his expense accounts.

When this was finally made clear to him, and he had honestly and fully repented his old infidelity, he was at last able to feel released. His sense of guilt left him. His anxiety about his expense account, which had been morbid, disappeared.

The mind can play many deceptive, baffling tricks, but none can cause more anguish than a sense of guilt which expresses itself in a masked, disguised form.

It is our destiny, as human beings, to pass judgment on ourselves. A sense of right and wrong, of good and evil, is as basic to our nature as are the forces of love and hate. As human beings, we are bound to realize that there is a difference between right and wrong. As inevitably as a river flows to the sea, we are compelled by an inner necessity to attempt to abide by some code of ethics, whatever it may be. But, as human beings, we are also prone to moral lapses. We are able neither to conquer every temptation that comes our way, nor to escape self-condemnation when we fail. No one can violate his own ethical principles, the precepts of his religion, and not suffer guilt feelings, consciously or unconsciously.

To enable troubled people to get at the hidden roots of an unresolved guilt feeling is one of psychiatry's chief contributions to the cure of emotional and physical ills.

And so it is an absolute rule of successful living that one must be able to feel forgiven, even though he has done wrong, if he seeks God's forgiveness and his own as well, and if he is truly sorry for his act. To press on with a mind clear of a sense of guilt, time must be permitted to close over the past and the energies must be concentrated on the present. Only so are we able to live at peace with ourselves.

The Bible says that we are "saved through faith." That is, salvation comes to us by asking forgiveness through our faith in God and then having the faith to believe that it is granted; for otherwise old failures and sins become an intolerable load that weighs us down so that our best energies, which should be used to meet today's problems, are spent repenting yesterday's failures.

Many years ago, Sir William Osler, the great pioneer in medical science, gave a lecture called "The Way of Life." In this he told his audience that before they tried to learn anything else they should learn this one thing—*Live one day at a time*.

He described how an ocean liner is built so that the captain can, by pressing a button, lower steel doors separating one watertight bulkhead from another. If the hull is pierced in a disaster, this keeps the ship afloat. In the voyage of life, Osler advised, learn how to make doors come down and shut out the yesterdays with all their errors and failures. Learn also to lower another door to shut out the unborn tomorrows so that you can live for this day alone. As you move into the next bulkhead, close doors that will shut out both the past and the future.

But at our clinic we constantly see people who have been made incapable of following this wise counsel. Why? Because their past errors darken the present and bring a constant dread of the future. Because forgiveness has not been theirs! And so they carry around with them their whole lives all the mistakes they have ever made.

Generally they have repented time and time again, but all without result. They continue to flay themselves with an old and seemingly deathless conviction of wrongdoing. Typically, they have come to regard their sins as beyond forgiveness by God or man. They often magnify petty transgressions into major ones. They suffer torments of anxiety, and they hate themselves as inferior and unworthy. Sometimes they even have accidents in order, unconsciously, to punish themselves.

Their difficulty is that the true, complete cause of their guilt feelings is hidden from them in their unconscious minds. And for them, the harmonious teamwork of religion and psychiatry is particularly effective. The depth psychology of psychiatry has charted in detail the subtle dynamics by which guilt feelings are kept from one's full awareness. By demonstrating to a person the true source of his feeling of guilt, the psychiatrist can often enable him to do that which he could not do before, deal directly with it. The submerged guilt is brought out into the open. Then religious guidance by the minister can be brought to bear. Healing forgiveness, so long and painfully denied, at last becomes possible.

Let us illustrate this. A devoutly religious woman, married and with two sons, suffered for years from increasingly severe feelings of guilt. They centered on an indiscretion which had occurred more than twenty-five years previously. Before she married her husband she had been engaged to another man whom she loved desperately. On one occasion she allowed him to have sexual relations with her. A short while after this, without giving any explanation, he brutally broke off the engagement.

Memories of that early sexual experience became an obsession with her. She confessed to her minister who prayed with her and told her that she was forgiven by God. But it was to no avail, because she could not forgive herself. She repeated the confession several times. And still her guilt persisted with all its unrelenting force. She was highly nervous, lost weight, and was unable to sleep.

Psychiatric study uncovered her trouble. She respected her husband, but she did not love him as much, or so she imagined, as she did the man to whom she was previously engaged. Without realizing it, she was still in love with the first man and wanted him back. And here is the critical point: in her unconscious mind she kept right on committing, over and over, the same old sin, as her fantasies and dreams showed.

Since she did not know this, she did not really repent it; and not having repented, naturally, she could not feel forgiven. But once she understood this mechanism that was frustrating her happiness, it no longer had such a hold over her.

Now she could be helped by the minister. He gave her a precise "prescription" to follow. She was to do the following things three times each day: First, she was urged to remember that this man to whom she had been engaged had treated her very unworthily; he did not deserve her affection. And so she was to separate herself from him in her mind. Second, she was to realize that this man whom she had known so long ago was now greatly changed and possibly even unattractive. If she were to see him now she would probably be astonished that she ever had any love for him. All that remained was a fantasy about him to which there was doubtless no substance. Third, she was to remind herself that she really loved her husband with whom she had lived in a good relationship all of these years. Fourth, she was to remind herself that if a person sincerely and contritely asks God to forgive, He always forgives; therefore she had been forgiven, whether she felt it or not, and no guilt remained in her. And in order to confirm these feelings, she was to repeat the following passages of Scripture:

"He hath not dealt with us after our sins; nor rewarded us according to our iniquities. For as the heaven is high above the earth, so great is His mercy toward them that fear Him. As far as the east is from the west, so far hath He removed our transgressions from us." And, ". . . though your sins be as scarlet, they shall be as white as snow."

Finally, she was to give thanks that the Lord had taken the other man from her and given her such an understanding husband. She was to thank God constantly that for all these years she had had a husband who respected her and loved her and had never harmed her, but only worked for her good.

Her story—and when she left she was a new, radiant person—proves once more that self-knowledge is the first step toward self-control. It was when she understood that she was unconsciously harboring thoughts and desires contrary to her ideals that she could intelligently ask forgiveness and be conscious of having received it. And it was only then, too, that she could forgive herself.

Feelings of guilt which are hidden, and therefore unresolved, can spread their poison with undiminished strength year after year. Psychiatry, searching for an answer to this strange fact, has found it through the analysis of the way in which a person's earliest ideas of right and wrong are formed.

The process of shaping our moral concepts begins practically at birth. We have an innate, God-given capacity for self-criticism, but of course at first this is only a seed, a potentiality. Its growth is profoundly influenced during infancy and childhood in a special way.

A small child is sharply sensitive to his parents' attitudes, to their criticisms of him. He wants to avoid being scolded and punished or, worse still, losing their affection. And so he wants to obey them. But his strong desires and his curiosity about his new world lead him into activities that crash head on against his parents' notions of how he should behave.

Only the wisest mother and father can help him solve this conflict successfully. It requires the patience of an angel, a virtue very few people have. And sometimes stern discipline may seem a simpler way out than patient understanding. For instance, a child asks blunt questions about sex or meets his physical needs in a primitive fashion. If his parents respond with harsh commands, or unexplained prohibitions, perhaps because they are nervous, or irritable, or honestly perplexed, then the child may be frightened, or bewildered. His feelings are confused about his own behavior, particularly about various bodily functions which are the object of the most strict, and often to him incomprehensible, tabus and regulations.

Parents, well intentioned though they may be, also frequently give their children the idea that all sex is wrong or even wicked. And so this function becomes inhibited. More than one marriage has foundered on the reef of sexual inhibitions unwittingly instilled during childhood.

The child may, too, be confused by his parents' reception of his childish fantasies. For example, a five-year-old boy told his father he was late for supper because he met a bear in the woods on his way home.

"Well," his father asked, "what did you do?"

"Oh, I just opened my mouth and swallowed him."

The little boy was sent to bed supperless. The father only meant to teach him not to "tell lies." But from this and similar incidents, the child got the idea, which persisted all through his life, that there was something wrong about all imagination.

If, as a child grows up, he acquires rigid ideas of what is right or wrong, he will say to himself, "I've been bad. My father will certainly punish me." And so he begins to know the meaning of guilt, and of fear of punishment by an implacable authority. He accepts his parents' judgment blindly.

His budding capacity for criticism of his own behavior

has been sharpened and molded by the impact of his parents' criticism of him. And then the child actually absorbs into his own deeper mind the critical attitudes of his mother and father. They become a lasting part of his inner self-censoring mechanism. It is as though, for all his life, whenever he has to make a decision, a warning parental voice echoes out of the past, or rather, from his unconscious mind, where it is now permanently lodged.

The sound, correctly understood ideas he received from his parents become a part of this inner self-censorship also; but, unfortunately, so do all his false, misunderstood ideas of right and wrong. And if he saw his parents as harsh and punishing, his own critical faculties, into which their attitudes are now incorporated, will make him as strict with himself as he fancied they were.

As a child grows up his early moral concepts have to be modified, reinterpreted and matured in line with his experience in an expanding adult world. Other voices of authority add to what his parents have taught him. Friends and associates whose opinions he especially values, and his church and his school, complete the molding of his ideals and principles.

A person whose unconscious mind is crammed with mistaken, falsely conceived attitudes may still achieve for himself an adult moral code, but he will find it hard to live by. He accepts it intellectually, but not in his deepest mind. He is trying to regulate his life by two contradictory sets of rules: one adult, one infantile.

Certain feelings may be so charged with old, guilty associations that his harsh inner censor keeps them from reaching consciousness, but he suffers for them just the same. It is characteristic that he will have a concept of God as just as stern and unforgiving as his parents once were.

Such a person is in trouble, although by no means hopelessly so. Those repressed feelings and thoughts can be brought to the surface where they can be re-evaluated in the light of reasoned judgment. Then he can be guided to forgiveness, to a new idea of God, a God who is loving, and compassionate, and who regards all of us as His children.

A young man who came to the clinic had had instilled in him from childhood an apprehensive feeling about sex. His mother kept warning him that he must never bring disgrace on the family. And her idea of the worst possible disgrace was being discovered in a sexual indiscretion. It was an obsession with her. Buy why?

In the small town where she had been brought up, the father of one of her closest friends had become involved in a notorious extramarital affair. Under the community's rigid moral standards, his whole family felt publicly humiliated. She could never forget the suffering he made them endure, nor her fear of some such scandal developing in her own family. To her mind it became the most awful thing that could happen to a human being. This obsession dominated her when she was young, and later, her relationship with her own children.

As might be expected, her son reacted negatively to this hysterical counseling. He finally left home and then he plunged into one sexual excess after another. One day he brought himself up short. He said to himself, "You have now done just what your mother told you not to do! You have opened up the possibility of disgracing your whole family." And he began to live in terror that he would be found out and exposed.

Finally he went to a minister and confessed, asking for forgiveness time and time again, but he could achieve no peace. On the one hand his conscious, reasoning mind, and his religion, told him that he could be forgiven. But on the other hand, his unconscious mind, his inner censor, told him that his sins were too terrible to be wiped off the slate.

He could not reconcile this conflict, and he fell into a panic. His imagination summoned up the most horrible punishments. He feared he would have a fatal accident, or lose all his money, or die suddenly of a heart attack. His childish sense of guilt took many forms, but they all resulted from the old, haunting fear that, having done wrong, he would be found out and something terrible would happen.

He was finally convinced that his trouble lay in his unconscious mind; that his mother, without intending to, had transmitted to him her own neurotic attitudes about sex, which were many and deep, and that these were still operating deep within him. He should not love or respect her any the less, but he should understand her as a human being as well as a mother. And he was slowly helped to give up his warped ideas and to develop a healthy and balanced and Christian attitude toward morals.

A pastor helped him to see that people frequently take a morbid view of sins of the flesh. Women, especially, are taught that this is the primary sin. "And yet," the pastor said, "when we study the teachings of Jesus we note that he stressed the sins of the spirit quite as emphatically as the sins of the flesh."

He went on: "And you remember the beautiful story of the prodigal son. In this parable the son asked the father for his inheritance and then went to a distant land and wasted it in riotous living. Finally penniless, he wandered about the countryside eating with pigs and sleeping in stables. Then he 'came to himself.' He saw the error of his ways, repented, and went back home.

"His father saw him afar off and ran out to meet him with love and compassion. He said, 'My son was dead, and is alive again; he was lost, and is found.' The father didn't chide his son or remind him of the wrong he had done. His boy had discovered that for himself the hard way. The mere fact that he was returning in humility revealed the depth and sincerity of his repentance. So the father, out of a heart of love, forgave him."

The pastor added that, although no feeling of guilt should be ignored, yet when forgiven it is extremely foolish to go on suffering about it. He suggested that the boy say to himself several times each day, "God has been very good to me. He has forgiven every wrong I ever did. God no longer remembers my sins; therefore I am forgetting them, also." He was to repeat this until it no longer was necessary.

Then, one day, he discovered that he had forgotten to say it! He found that he had not been disturbed about the memory of his transgressions for months. Gradually they grew dimmer and dimmer until finally they were buried in the past. They had lost their power over him.

A person dominated by an infantile, cruel inner censorship over his emotions and acts can, we repeat, never forgive himself. In this way he violates Christ's teachings by placing himself outside of God's saving grace. He is apt not only to suffer mentally, but even to inflict physical punishment on himself for his sins, real or imagined. This may take strange forms.

He may, for example, actually be led into antisocial acts. In studying crime, psychiatrists have found much to indicate that the real, although hidden, motive is frequently an overwhelming compulsion to be punished. For instance, children who steal very often do so because they prefer to be punished for theft rather than for their primitive, unconscious desires, their "secret sins," which they are unable to face.

Criminals are very prone to leave behind them unwittingly some kind of evidence which will lead to their arrest and punishment. In many cases, it seems clear, criminals actually want to be caught and punished for what they have done. It is their twisted way of getting relief from inner feelings of guilt that they are unable to deal with openly and directly.

Much the same kind of mental mechanism causes many, perhaps most, accidents. Accidents in which the person responsible is injured are, in psychiatry's view, generally a form of self-inflicted punishment for an unconscious sense of guilt. During the last war a nineteen-year-old boy was brought into a hospital with a multiple fracture of his right leg. He had ridden on his bicycle out onto the highway, on the wrong side of the road and without looking. He was hit by an oncoming truck. He had no explanation for his carelessness. He insisted that he was always very cautious, and that this was the first accident he had ever had.

Eventually a psychiatrist uncovered pertinent, and revealing facts. Some weeks before his accident the boy, on his mother's insistence, had asked his draft board to exempt him, on the grounds that he was needed on the farm, since his father could not do all the work alone. The board granted his request.

But although his exemption followed the letter of the

law, the boy could not accept it as being quite legitimate. His brother, who was in the marines, had been badly wounded in the South Pacific, and he wanted to join the marine corps himself. In his unconscious mind, he felt that his own behavior was wrong and unjustified. Without being aware of what he was doing, he had had the accident to punish himself; and, since his mother now had to take care of him, she, too, was punished for her complicity in his draft evasion.

Another case in point is that of a woman who broke her hip twice within five years. The second time she became depressed and uneasy, because she felt there was something peculiar about these accidents. The feeling became so strong, and so disturbing to her, that she finally came to the clinic.

She told the counselor that after she had been married for about thirty years her husband fell ill. He soon became a complete invalid, and since she could not afford a professional nurse, she had to care for him almost constantly. One day she found out that his illness was due to syphilis, which he had contracted before he had married her. This discovery was a tremendous shock to her. It filled her with resentment and hatred.

These emotions were so powerful that she even wished he would die. But instead of bringing them out into the open, perhaps talking to her physician or to her minister about them, she tried to wipe them out of her mind because they were so disturbing to her.

One day, about five years after her husband fell ill, she spent the morning waxing the living room floor. When the doorbell rang, she ran to answer it, slipped on the newly waxed floor, and broke her hip. About a year later her husband died. And shortly afterward she repeated the accident in exactly the same way. She waxed the living room floor, ran to answer the doorbell, fell and broke the same hip, in the same spot.

It was not difficult for her to comprehend that her accidents occurred because of her hatred toward her husband, and toward his memory. She was a curious combination of a devoted and yet a hating wife, who could solve her internal conflict only by punishing herself. The first thing she had to do was to understand this quite clearly, and then to set about freeing herself of the self-castigating attitudes that were so dangerous to her.

One day her pastor pointed out to her, "You have no reason to hate yourself. If you had been a less kindly human being you might have left your husband at once when you found out about his condition. But you didn't. You accepted your sense of obligation to him, and cared for him tenderly. Isn't that true?"

Her face lost some of its troubled look. "Yes," she admitted, "I did do that."

"In other words, you exercised a full and Christian duty, didn't you? You did the best you could in a difficult situation."

She admitted that despite her anger toward her husband she had treated him in a kindly and sympathetic way. She began to see that she had been more of a Christian than she had thought herself to be. It gave her a new sense of self-respect that opened the door of her mind to more wholesome beliefs about herself.

"What must I do now?" she asked.

"Do this," the pastor said. "Ask God to forgive you for any wrong you may have committed, or any wrong you think you may have committed. Having asked for forgiveness, believe that you will receive it, now. It is, actually, all in the past, but you must believe that it is in the past and no longer with you.

"Each day repeat to yourself half a dozen times this wise counsel from the Scriptures, 'forgetting those things which are behind, and reaching forth unto those things which are before.' Each morning when you get up, say to yourself, 'My life has started afresh and I thank God for His goodness in giving me a new and happy start in a life which I shall make useful to all those with whom I come in contact.' "

Another disguise, in which a submerged sense of guilt shows itself, is that all too common malady of the spirit, a chronic feeling of inferiority, which is popularly known as an "inferiority complex." Everyone is familiar with the symptoms. The sufferer is forever running himself down, belittling himself, underestimating his abilities, and feeling sure that he will be unable to do what is asked of him. Sometimes he covers all of this with a superlative degree of bumptiousness, but most often the feeling of inferiority is obvious.

Offered a job, or any opportunity, he is apt to say, "Oh, I'm afraid not. I'd better not try to do that. I'm not up to it. Better get someone with more brains, or experience, than I have."

The self-belittling has gone on until his mind has accepted his own evaluation of himself. He is not going to rise any higher in achievement than he himself is convinced is possible. As the Scriptures say, "According to your faith shall it be done unto you." And no one can go any higher than he believes is possible way down in his own heart.

Such a person is hypercritical of himself but at the same time extreme hypersensitive to criticism from anyone else. He lives in awe of every authority, just as he once lived in fear of criticism or punishment by the first authority in his life, his parents.

His plight can be seen in the caricature Caspar Milquetoast, The Timid Soul, drawn by the famous cartoonist, Webster. In a typical drawing, Webster shows him holding a Christmas present in his hand. One label on the box reads, "Perishable"; the other, "Do not open until Christmas." The Timid Soul, totally unnerved by these contradictory instructions, is symbolic of all too many people.

An excessive sense of inferiority makes him feel "he is damned if he does and damned if he doesn't." It paralyzes action and robs him of what he could accomplish if his real, but pent-up, capacities were released. It leads to perfectionist standards, because his powers of self-criticism are so sharp. And, since they are based on childish ideas, so unrealistic that he feels he must be perfect in order to escape condemnation, naturally, such perfection being impossible, he continually falls short of his overidealistic goals. This, then, magnifies his feeling of unworthiness and the circle starts over.

To understand this person is to understand the whole

theory of what a deeply repressed emotion can do. He is the victim of training in excessive self-criticism and of impossibly high standards of behavior. He may be victimized by his unconscious hatred, or by mistaken ideas about sexuality in marriage, mistaking his normal instincts for bestiality. And he has a sick and misdirected conscience which represses his feelings and emotions and allows them to fester inside his mind. The result is a feeling of guilt, of self-belittling, of loathing, that robs him of most of his effectiveness in life, along with his happiness.

But these judgments of himself are on an infantile basis. He has failed to mature, and this failure brings him into conflict with the Bible's precept, as expressed by St. Paul, "When I was a child, I spake as a child, I understood as a child, I thought as a child; but when I became a man, I put away childish things." And he is certainly unable to carry out the true meaning of Christ's injunction to "love thy neighbor as thyself," for if a man's esteem for himself is a poor, weak thing, his love for his fellow man will be no better.

We are not, naturally, advocating here a blind, arrogant self-love. That is as unhealthy as inferiority, and, incidentally, often has the same basis. The goal must be a properly humble, but accurately realistic, estimation of his own worth. Either extreme of feeling about one's self is almost always unjustified by fact.

When Mr. C., as we will call him, came to us, he was a beaten man, old before his time, primarily because of his extreme lack of faith in himself. His accomplishments and good qualities belied his low opinion of himself. Typically, logic carried little weight with him. He was a handsome man, intelligent, even brilliant, but he had, nevertheless, a most profound sense of insecurity and inadequacy. He had done well in his business, where he was financially successful because, for the most part, he had had to deal with only one or two people at a time. But when he had to talk at a meeting he trembled, stammered, and broke out into a cold sweat, and he would lose track of his thoughts even though he had started out with an orderly, well formed idea.

He was particularly fearful of other men. He felt inferior to them and yet at the same time was infuriated when he was surpassed by them in any way. It made him sick with envy, for example, if another man had a better car, or a more expensive house. He was uneasy in his own office, and certain that his colleagues were antagonistic to him. He worried that important contracts would be canceled, and was certain everything was going to work out for the worst.

In short, despite his business success and the material advantages that it brought him, his life seemed more uncomfortable and more difficult than he could bear.

In his childhood, Mr. C. had regarded his father, who was one of the great trial lawyers of his day, with awe and terror. His earliest memories were of being bullied and ridiculed by his father, who probably meant only to tone down his child's egotism, but overdid it to a destructive extent. He would tell him that he talked too much, or too little. He accused him of being stupid, or of acting as if he knew everything. The boy eventually got the idea there was no way he could please his father; everything he did was wrong in one way or another.

He recalled, and he trembled when he did so, an occasion when, at the age of four, he wet his bed. His father slapped him, scolded him and frightened him so violently that even when he grew up the unconscious memory of his fright blocked off this natural function whenever other men were present. It was clear he still had an unconscious terror that his father would appear, with angry eyes and flushed face, as he had so long ago, to punish him.

Mr. C. realized that he felt anger and resentment toward his father, but he had no idea of the intensity of these emotions. They were so frightening that his inner censor kept them for the most part locked in the depths of his mind. The guilt they caused, the fear of punishment for hating his father so savagely, reached awareness only as anxiety, and as a conviction of his own unworthiness.

A person must be able to express such feelings of aggression in a specific way, for the specific purpose of getting rid of them. And so, during many hours, Mr. C. was helped to unravel the memories of his early life until he could bring his feeling back into consciousness. Eventually, and without fear or shame, he was able to pour out the fury which had been bottled up for so long. The mental catharsis slowly exposed and drained off the hidden rage, so that it could be dealt with rationally.

It was like the story in the Bible of the person's mind that was haunted by evil spirits which were all swept away. But, he was reminded, the Bible says, that if something else did not take their place, they would steal back. What Mr. C. would have to do now was to tenant his emptied mind with creative, wholesome thoughts. The only therapy which could finally cure him was the therapy of love. He must forgive his father, understand and reject all of his resentment, and then put into practice a Christian love for him. We suggested that he do some specific kindly acts for his father: go and see him, pray for him, send him gifts. We suggested that he should make a list of all the kindly things his father had undoubtedly done for him. Above all, he should treat his father, consciously, as one adult treats another, and not as a child treats an adult.

In these ways he would heal the hurt in his own soul and, once he should begin to feel at home with his new attitudes, he might get a different concept of what his father really was like. Perhaps he would eventually be able to see that his father was only a fallible human being who may easily have had a similar unhappiness in his own childhood.

Gradually, as he followed the technique we outlined for him, his feelings toward his father did change. And, as his attitude toward his father changed, so did his attitude toward himself. The old angers and grievances began to resolve and, along with them, the feelings of guilt and inferiority.

No one has to let errors of the past destroy his present or cloud his future. The glorious fact is we can always have a new beginning. Naturally, a wise person will try to avoid feelings of guilt by avoiding the acts that cause them. He will look and exercise his moral judgment, before he leaps. He will develop for himself a capacity for previewing his behavior in the light of what he knows to be right and wrong. But if he does something wrong, he must accept his errors frankly and then make an effort to obtain God's forgiveness. He should be able, although perhaps only with help, to recognize his error, ask forgiveness for it, and make restitution if that be possible. Then he can go his way with an untroubled mind.

If, despite everything, a sense of guilt, or of unjustified inferiority, still persists, he should seek advice from a specialist in psychiatric counseling and from the pastor. It is probable that either he has not sufficiently re-educated his unconscious mind, or that the cause of his feelings is not clear to him. As long as these buried, and generally disguised, guilt feelings are not brought out into the light of reason, they rot the fiber of the spirit. They prohibit the acceptance of one's heritage of God's love and forgiveness.

It is true that the way of the transgressor is hard, hard as flint. And because it is so hard, Christ came in order to tell what can be done about it. When a man confesses his sins to Jesus Christ, something happens to him: the weight is lifted, taken away, and he lives as he never lived before.

"I live; yet not I, but Christ liveth in me." The sins of the past are erased, gone and forgotten. A man becomes a new creature. This is the most marvelous thing in the world.

Sometimes when people come to us because they are unable to forgive themselves for their past mistakes, we tell them the story of St. Paul. Before St. Paul was converted to Christianity, he was a violent opponent of Christ's followers. He made it his business to hunt them down and to stone, torture and imprison them. As the Bible says, "He made havoc of the church."

But one day he saw the light and became converted. The man who was such a ferocious enemy of Christ became one of his greatest followers. And when he had repented his sins—and they were grievous and many—he was able to receive and to accept wholeheartedly God's forgiveness. After a life of tumult he could say with serene confidence, "I have fought a good fight, I have finished my course, I have kept the faith." The past was gone and forgotten. He was at peace with himself.

We should never allow ourselves to be overwhelmed by past mistakes. God never meant us to carry around our necks the millstones of old misdeeds. We can be free of a sense of guilt about them. We can move, clear-eyed, with a buoyant heart and mind, toward a successful future. The moving, triumphant story of St. Paul gives courage and abiding hope to all who have felt their sins too heavy to be lifted.

IV Relax and renew joyous power

Gilbert Dodds, one of the greatest track stars of our time, crouched at the starting line of the Wanamaker mile run. The flying parson, as the sports writers call him, took that brief moment to say a silent prayer. Letting his body relax in preparation for the tremendous effort to come, he prayed, "Oh Lord, in this glorious sport I pray that you will let me run well. Help each man running against me to do his best, too. Go along with each of us. Amen." He did not beseech God to let him win. He prayed for them all, his competitors as well as himself.

At the starting gun, Dodds swung into his beautiful rhythmic stride. Every nerve and muscle in his body seemed to be working together in perfect harmony. He gave the impression that if challenged he had resources of power, an extra strength, that would bring him victory. Free of any stress, moving ahead with an effortless grace, he went out in front of his competitors and came home an easy winner. Gil Dodds knew that a relaxed body and a quiet mind turned toward God can indeed draw on deep reserves of power when they are most needed. This is a lesson in successful living too few of us have ever learned.

Dr. Flanders Dunbar, an authority on psychosomatic medicine, writes in her book, *Mind and Body,* "The inability to relax is one of the most widely spread diseases of our time and one of the most infrequently recognized." Our experience confirms this. There do not seem to be many people who understand the absolute necessity of relaxing, or who would know how to practice that re-creating art if they tried.

At our Marble Collegiate Church clinic we have worked out some simple and practical methods of relax-ation. They have brought joy and peace of mind to hundreds of troubled men and women. And these tech-niques studied and applied will do the same thing for oth-ers.

Those who come to us for help with their problems fre-quently complain that today is the most wearing, madden-ing period in which man ever tried to live. The pressures, the complications of contemporary life, they exclaim, are enough to "drive anyone out of his mind." And as they describe their almost constant worries and anxieties, they seem to affirm the truth of what Thoreau wrote long ago: "The mass of men lead lives of quiet desperation."

It could be debated whether the difficulties that beset this generation are any worse than those of earlier times. But it must be admitted that the troubles of our own day are brought home to us in a way they never were before. Our remarkably efficient radio, newsreels and press, and all of those organizations which are the triumph of the American free access to news inform us well. But they are also apt to agitate us daily with a host of explosive, nerve-shattering reports.

Many a morning that starts off placidly enough is ruined by the breakfast reading of the paper. Details of crimes, of disasters, of international incidents, or of na-tional or local politics and politicians, shatter all tranquil-ity. Nerves become jangled; muscles tighten. Before the last sip of coffee is gulped down an old suspicion has been reawakened: the nation and the world are going to the dogs!

Add to this sort of thing the haunting, shadowy fears caused by hostilities, and guilt feelings rising up from the unconscious mind; then add the worries and irritations of personal and business life; and you have a sure formula for that all too common malady, tension.

But why do we do all of this worrying? Actually, although most of our worries serve little purpose beyond upsetting us, we find them hard to give up. In the *Reader's Digest,** the noted humorist, Frank Sullivan, presents his recipe for a nervous breakdown.

"Find out what kind of worry suits your temperament and then stick to it," Sullivan writes. "Personally, I like to track down some absurd little tribulation, nurse it along and build it up into a fine, upstanding disaster. It appeals to the creative artist in me to mail a letter and then start worrying over whether I put a stamp on it or addressed it correctly—until I'm a wreck. . . . And don't neglect your health as a subject. You may think you are well now, but the chances are you are coming down with something at this very moment." And he solemnly advises, "Let no day pass without crying over some spilt milk, even if you have to spill it yourself just to keep your hand in."

In his droll way, Sullivan has pointed out a great truth about human nature: that most of us do seem determined to find something to worry about. Did I make a bad impression at that meeting, a person anxiously asks himself, or will I at the next one? Will my boy pass his school examinations? Something might happen to my husband's job. What if there is a depression? Suppose I don't get that raise, how will I meet the payments on the house? There are all the things that could have happened, and the things that might, and the things that never will. Many worries, of course, are based on real difficulties that have to be solved in one definite way or another. But the confirmed worrier generally puts more energy into fretting about his troubles than in trying to solve them.

Then there are a whole procession of minor irritations to keep one agitated. We once asked a man who complained of feeling tired all the time, even when he was "resting," to write down all the incidents that got on his nerves in a single week. The list he brought us later, and it went on for pages, included these items:

The honking of the horn of a car held up in traffic . . .

* Originally published in *Good Housekeeping*.

a telephone call cut off in the middle of a sentence ... he couldn't find his favorite tie ... a garage door which wouldn't open ... his wife criticized his bridge game ... a bus conductor refused to change a five dollar bill ... his favorite dessert was crossed off the menu ... children screamed in the street outside his window ... the radio blared next door ... a salesman was too busy to wait on him ... a couple sitting behind him in the movies talked incessantly, and the woman three rows in front wore a plumed hat ... a friend was less loyal than he expected ... a policeman bawled him out for overparking ... a woman's stories bored him, and she wouldn't listen to his ...

Although this man was no crank, but just an ordinary human being, the list went on and on, and as he looked at it he had to smile, a little ruefully. He was amazed to discover how often in a single day he was exasperated by something that his judgment told him was petty, and yet which, as he put it, "nearly drove me crazy."

It would indeed be a fortunate person who could rise above all the minor annoyances of daily life; a doubly fortunate one who could avoid all frustration, with its attending anger and resentment, by achieving all his goals, or not worrying when he did not. Very few of us are up to this! And so most of us, to a greater or lesser degree, are victims not only of anxiety, but also of a wearing, exhausting muscular tension. Without quite realizing it, we yearn for relief from this painful state as avidly as a desert wanderer thirsts for water. Yet the secret of gaining such relief can be learned by anyone.

A young man in his mid-twenties came to our clinic in a sadly wrought-up state. He felt guilty about his past and apprehensive about his future. He had just gone through the misery of a broken marriage which was only the culmination of several unfortunate incidents in his life. At the moment he suffered from the most painful feelings of anger at his wife for having left him and at himself because he sensed it was not entirely her fault.

The minister saw that he was intensely perturbed, restless and fretful. He spoke soothingly to him for a few minutes and then asked him to sit back in his chair. "Pretend," he suggested, "that you weigh three hundred pounds, that you are so heavy you cannot support your own weight. Let your body bear down on the chair, resting heavily against it. Let your head fall back, close your eyes, rest your hands limply on the arms of the chair.

"Now," the pastor said, "when you feel completely relaxed, take five or six deep breaths. Don't hurry it. Do it slowly. Take it easy."

Then he asked the young man to think of his mind as becoming quiet and still. "As long as the surface of your mind is agitated," he said, "deeper, more peaceful thoughts, cannot rise up to calm it. If we can get the surface of your mind serene for even a few minutes, thoughts will rise from its depths that will spread their peace over you."

When he saw that the young man's body was in a state of relaxation, he began quietly to recite passages from the Scriptures. He repeated the lovely words from Isaiah, "Thou wilt keep him in perfect peace, whose mind is stayed on Thee." He talked to him about this marvelous statement, and how one is kept in perfect peace if he keeps his mind fixed, not on his troubles, but on God. Another verse he recited was, "Come unto Me, all ye that labor and are heavy laden, and I will give you rest." And again, "Peace I leave with you, My peace I give unto you. . . . Let not your heart be troubled, neither let it be afraid."

As the soothing, healing words went on and on, the young man began to yield to them, until he experienced the magic touch of peace itself. As the pastor put it, the hand of the Great Physician rested on him, extracting the mass of disturbing thoughts from his mind. It was a deliverance from inner agitation; it was the gift of peace! Presently he declared that he felt rested and refreshed.

Here was a demonstration of what is promised in the Twenty-third Psalm, "He restoreth my soul." That is exactly what happened. His soul—that is, he himself—was restored.

The minister told him how Roger Babson, the famous statistician, had once said that he practiced breathing in the peace of God and breathing out all tension and worries. "You can learn to do that," the minister said. And he advised the young man to repeat the method of relaxation three times a day. And as he did so he was to say to himself such Scriptural passages as those previously suggested, which he had committed to memory.

Later this young man reported that he had followed the pastor's prescription faithfully. As a result his whole outlook changed. "I have learned," he said gratefully, "the secret of having peace of mind and feel confident that I can now go ahead and solve my own problems."

Relaxation of mind and body go together. For, as neurologists tell us, our minds and bodies are constantly acting upon each other. To illustrate, whenever a person has a craving for something, impulses sent from the brain along various nerves stimulate muscles in order to satisfy that craving. The person's feelings, in turn, depend on whether or not the muscular action succeeds in its purpose.

Let us take a simple illustration of this. A hungry baby puckers up his mouth and moves his hands toward the bottle. Then another set of muscles carries the milk down his throat and through his whole digestive system. An adult goes through a more complicated set of muscular reactions to hunger. His legs carry him to the table, his arms and hands put the food in his mouth and he then swallows and digests it.

When hunger is satisfied, all these muscles relax and at the same time there is a pleasant feeling of contentment. The fed baby gurgles happily. The well fed adult shows his relaxation and contentment by leaning back, and emanating a general satisfaction with the world. And, incidentally, it is now and not before that a sensible colleague brings up that matter they had agreed to discuss at luncheon.

But if the hunger craving is not satisfied, the result is very different. If the muscles are balked, unable to carry through the motions which have been started by the nerve impulses, they take on a certain amount of tension. And along with this tension go resentment and anger. A baby whose hunger is unsatisfied yells his resentment lustily. The ravenous adult, whose luncheon has been delayed, shows his anger by being nervous and short-tempered.

Very much the same process goes on even when our cravings, our goals, are far more complex than hunger or thirst. We want to be successful in business, to write a book, to climb a mountain, to be loved, to become a doctor, to make a speech, to do anything on which we have set our hearts. The formula still applies. Ambitions, as well as simple cravings, set in motion complicated nerve-muscle actions. If we succeed, there is relaxation and contentment. If we fail, and are frustrated, there is muscle tension accompanied by anger and by anxiety. The three emotions of love, hate, and fear, like the three primary colors from which all the hues of the rainbow are mixed, are the basic ingredients of all human feelings.

Over the years people develop more or less characteristic ways of responding to situations, and, through constant repetition, their tensions become written into their bodies. They reveal these muscle tensions, and their typical patterns of emotional responses, in their posture, by the way in which they walk and sit, in the lines of their faces, and in the pitch and volume of their voices.

We may not always be aware of our own fundamental tensions, but we do react almost instinctively to those of other people. For these tensions are registered not only in their faces, but in their whole bodies, and reflect their emotional attitudes. It is in this way that we very often form our idea of what another person is really like.

A personnel director in a plant may, for instance, turn a man down for a job, not because of his lack of qualifications on paper, but because the personnel director gets an "impression" of unreliability. Sometimes one meets a person who is apparently kind, polite, and considerate, and yet who, because of his muscle tensions, is sensed to be a sham, and really full of suppressed anger and hostility. No one can hide his fundamental tensions, or the emotional pattern they express, entirely. And these old, long-standing, deeply implanted muscle tensions give a rigidity to the spirit and to the body as well.

When we look further into the relationship between the

mind and body we realize what a heavy price we pay, in physical energy, for that shadowy kind of fear known as anxiety.

Our nervous system was once little more than a group of fibers around the spinal cord. Then the hind brain developed, later the mid brain and finally the fore brain. It is the great fore brain that controls all the other nerve centers. If control by the fore brain is cut off, as it is in a stroke, for example, arm and leg muscles may become rigid. Or, where there is damage to the nerves running from this all-important fore brain, as in the disease known as palsy, the body becomes stiff, the face is masklike, the vocal cords contract, and the fingers twitch convulsively. Whenever there is any physical interference with the control of the fore brain over the lower nerve centers, the result is stiffness, contraction, lack of coordination and spasmodic movements.

Anxiety produces somewhat the same effect. Also, it partially blocks off the vitally necessary control by the fore brain. The lower, more primitive nerve centers take over. The whole body may become tense and rigid. You can see this, for example, in a man who is learning to drive a car. He is likely to hunch nervously forward, lunge at the brake or yank furiously at the wheel. His anxiety makes him throw every muscle in his body into the effort. After driving a few blocks he is worn out and limp. An experienced driver, free of anxiety, using only the muscles he needs, could drive from New York to Washington with less cost in energy.

Constant tension born of anxiety, anger, irritation, and frustration may lead to physical ailments. Even if it does not end in illness, the strain of tension, of which few of us are completely free, is exhausting and destructive to inner calm. We need, all of us, to find a way to break the deadly cycle of emotional upset: tension, heightened emotions, greater tension, until the cracking point is reached.

Naturally it often requires the aid of psychiatry to gain insight into the underlying causes of deep anxiety; and that may be the only way to be permanently rid of them. But learning how to relax will speed the process. There is no one, not even a person who thinks of himself as entirely free of conflict and tension, who will not benefit from a regularly practiced method of relaxation.

One of the most important steps in relaxation is to learn to think generously and truthfully. Thoughts of ill will, of guilt, of fear, produce tumult in the mind. On the contrary, thoughts of good will, trust, confidence, and goodness, create a spiritual calm and a bodily relaxation. Since thoughts tend to become automatic, healthful and healing thoughts deliberately repeated with persistent regularity will become natural, and constantly fill the mind with peace.

A man, a prominent lawyer in a big midwestern city, once told us how he had come upon this great truth. "I was on a business trip," he said, "and late one afternoon I returned to my hotel room in a jittery state. After I had washed up, I sat down and tried to write some letters, but I couldn't concentrate on them. I paced up and down the room, sat down, tried to read the paper, but it all just annoyed me! I decided I would go out and have a drink, do anything to get away from myself!

"As I was standing by the dresser my eye happened to fall on the Gideon Bible lying there. I had been in lots of hotel rooms and never opened one of those Bibles, but this time, on some strange impulse, I did. It so happened that the place to which I opened was one of the early Psalms, I think the seventeenth or eighteenth. I read a couple of them, and then I sat down and kept on reading.

"Pretty soon I came to the beautiful Twenty-third Psalm and I read the line which says, 'He leadeth me beside the still waters. He restoreth my soul.' And somehow that got me! It was just what I needed. So I kept on and, believe it or not, I lost myself completely in what I was reading.

"I finally closed the Book and sat still for a long time. Then I realized that I was completely relaxed. A strange sense of peace and rest had come over me. I felt as rested as though I had had a good night's sleep. The tension had, magically, been taken out of me. Previously I had been like a rubber band stretched to the limit. Now I felt easy and quiet, under control.

"And I thought to myself: 'If the Bible can do that for

me in one reading, then maybe if I read it every day and really make it a part of my life it might take away my nervousness entirely.' And, do you know, that's exactly what happened!"

The medicine of the Bible can help you to relax. Without any such experience in reading it, you might follow the example of the man we have just told you about. The Psalms are a good place to start. Begin with Psalm Number One and read a few of them, maybe not as many as he did. But then read some more the next day, and keep it up.

After the Psalms, start at the beginning of the New Testament and read through Matthew, Mark, Luke, and John. As you do so watch for sentences that have to do with peace, rest, quietness, and the presence of God.

Copy some of these passages on bits of paper or cards to put in the pocket. Then on a train or a bus, or whenever there are a few free moments, spend them committing these passages to memory. Let the words soak into the consciousness, literally saturate the thoughts. Gradually the mind will become peaceful and quiet, and the nerve strain will cease.

We repeat, the medicine of the Bible can help you relax. But like any other medicine, it works only when you take it.

There was a time when religion was regarded as something for Sunday or special occasions only. In their conversations most people, particularly men, are not likely to talk about religion. It is not natural to them and they are awkward about it. They can discuss politics, business, sports, or their neighbors freely, but they seem unable to discuss the greatest factor in human existence—the relationship between human beings and God. Yet that is changing! People are realizing that the religion they believe in is a practical thing, designed to help them in their everyday situations.

Sometimes one finds evidence of this in the most unexpected places. Here is an illustration. For many years May Ferris has been receptionist at the home office of the Bridgeport Brass Company, in Bridgeport, Connecticut. One day an employee requested that a Bible be placed in the reception room. Miss Ferris gave permission and soon a fine new Bible rested there on the table.

May Ferris delights in noticing how amazingly often callers now pick up the Bible to read in preference to magazines or other material. Frequently, she reports, someone who is interrupted to go inside the offices will stop on his return, look up the passage again, and finish it.

"You have no idea," she says, "how many people show their gratitude for the opportunity to read the Good Book in the middle of a busy day. I see changes in their expression as they close it, the disappearance of fret from their eyes—it's like a miracle." *

But, however you do it, wherever and whenever the opportunity arises, try to find some time each day for quiet contemplation that will revitalize your tense spirit. Find time to let yourself fall under the spell of God's healing power.

A man from Mobile, Alabama, once wrote to us to describe his own way of doing this. Occasionally, he said, when he feels nervous and irritable, he drives to the lovely shores of Mobile Bay. But real peace comes to him not from the contemplation of this natural beauty alone; he has what he calls his spiritual medicine chest, where, having stored up in his mind peace-filled sentences from the Scriptures, he draws them out and repeats them to himself as he sits by the bay's sloping shore.

One of his favorite passages is: "My presence shall go with thee, and I will give thee rest." And then he says quietly, "God, the Father Who giveth me the peace that passeth all understanding, is with me now and will be with me all day long."

Then he sits for half an hour, feeling the quieting touch of God's hand on his nerves, and on his mind, and on his heart. And then he goes back to his business strengthened and refreshed.

But you do not have to retire to the seashore! You can find relaxation even in the midst of the press and rush of

* From *Guideposts*, a magazine published by Guideposts Associates, Inc., Pawling, New York.

city life. As you walk along the streets on your way to luncheon or, perhaps, to keep an appointment, do not occupy your mind with your troubles but form the habit of saying in one way or another, "God is with me, He will see me through." And if you encounter difficulties, avoid falling into the old way of seeing only their negative aspect. Say to yourself: "The Lord is with me. With His strength, I will get through this situation successfully."

Many painters, writers, musicians, and other artists have found their own special way of taking time out from the strain of creative work. John Masefield, the one-time bartender who became Poet Laureate of the British Empire, did this by practicing what he called, "the getting of tranquillity." Every night when he came home he would lie on his bed, relax himself and then sing a hymn or recite a few lines of poetry. And then he would say quietly, "God is with me, God watches over me."

There are as many ways of filling one's self with the conviction of the presence of God, as there are people who need it.

At our clinic a technique has been perfected for relaxation, based on the fundamental laws of mind and body. It gives relief from this muscular tension and makes it possible to tap the deep, hidden energies of the unconscious mind. Finish reading this chapter, then put down your book and actually try it. Here is a wonderfully effective prescription:

1. Lie down on your bed, or on a comfortable couch.
2. Clench your hands and then open them wide. (Remember, if you want to relax any part of the body you must first exercise it.) Double up your fists and make circular motions with them to exercise the forearm muscles.
3. Bring your clenched fists up to your shoulders and then extend your arms, in order to exercise the upper arm muscles. Next, make circular motions with the shoulders.
4. Now imagine that the nerves in your arms have been severed, so that they are helpless and you no longer have control over them. The arms should be so com-

pletely limp that if someone picks them up their entire weight rests in his hands. This is a test of whether or not your arms are truly relaxed.

5. Stretch your toes toward your head, without moving the legs, and then extend them. This exercises the muscles of the lower legs.

6. Bring up one knee until it comes close to your chest, and then extend it. Then do the same with the other knee.

7. Sit up and put your foot on a chair. Pull your foot off the chair and let your leg bend at the knee as though it were hinged. Repeat with the other foot.

8. Sit up and lie back several times to exercise the abdominal muscles.

9. Raise your head from the pillow and let it fall back.

10. Now take several deep breaths and stretch. The diaphragm, which is the chief breathing muscle, is the body's safety valve. A deep breath contracts the diaphragm and when the breath is let out quickly it is relaxed and its tension is relieved.

11. Finally, conceive, for a short interval, of all your irritations, your fears, your worries, your resentments, as slipping away. Replace them with the most soothing and pleasing scene you can imagine. Recall some memory of the mountains, or of the ocean, of autumn in the country—brown fields, misty hills, a bobwhite calling, and the occasional whistle of a distant train.

Lie on the couch for fifteen minutes after taking these exercises, thinking about each part of the body that you have tried to reach, until you come to a deeper and deeper level of relaxation. When you reach this state, you may be sure you are reaching down into the creative depths of your unconscious. Here is a pool of strength! People accomplish unbelievable feats in times of crisis by tapping this reservoir of power. There is no reason why it cannot be done in ordinary times.

Aldous Huxley says in his book, *Grey Eminence,* that those who give themselves up to their unconscious "get an extraordinary accession of moral strength." And then he says, "The will of the person in whom God lives is relaxed and effortless because it is not his own will but a great river of force flowing through him from a sea of subliminal consciousness."

Many people who have mastered this technique of relaxation tell us that they have found it a helpful remedy for sleeplessness. The fact is that anxiety, tension and insomnia go hand in hand. Anxiety and tension, the enemies of sleep, fill a person's mind with black, rest-destroying thoughts. They make him twist and fidget.

In insomnia, the first thing to do is, of course, to try to avoid taking worries to bed. William A. Quayle, a Methodist Bishop, was once preaching about worry, and he said, "One night along about twelve o'clock I was sitting up worrying and the Lord came to me and said, 'Son, what are you doing?' I said, 'I'm sitting up worrying.' And the Lord said, 'Well now, my son, you go to bed and go to sleep and I'll sit up and worry the rest of the night for you."

If you are unable to sleep, instead of getting up, wandering about the house, reading, listening to the radio, or whatever you do at such times, try lying in bed and making a conscious effort to relax the body completely, in the ways we have suggested. Do not try, so much, to eliminate disturbing thoughts as to replace them with peaceful ones. A little practice, a little patience, will accomplish this.

Then say to yourself a prayer or a few verses of some poem, perhaps this one:

SLEEP

Come hither, Sleep. Let happier mortals gain
The full embrace of thy soft angel wing:
But touch me with thy wand, or hovering
Above mine eyelids sweep me with thy train.
　　　　　Publius Papinius Statius
　　　　　(Translated by W. F. Fyfe)

Your health, your happiness, your success at whatever you are doing, demand that you find some form of relief from strain. Put aside a quiet little time each day, a time free of cares and of the many little pinpricks of life and for those moments, at least, put the telephone and the radio out of reach. Make yourself comfortable in an easy chair or on a couch.

Then, in whatever way is most natural to you, make contact with your own inner self and with your God. And through this moment of relaxation you can, if you will only try, revive in yourself a joyous power.

V How to stay healthy under pressure

Some time ago a minister in our clinic received a call to visit a patient in one of New York City's big hospitals. When he walked into the room he realized that the man was a complete stranger. Somewhat puzzled, he said, "You sent for me?"

"That's right."

"I don't believe I know you."

"I know you," the patient said. "I've heard you preach several times. I asked you to come because I want you to get me out of this place."

The minister was even more puzzled. "You mean you're here against your will?"

"No." The patient shook his head. "I'm being given the medical care I need. I know that. As a matter of fact I am a physician myself. But you're the only kind of a doctor who can get me out of here once and for all."

"I'm sorry," the minister said, "but I still don't understand."

"Look," the patient said earnestly. "I've got a stomach ulcer. And do you know how I got it? By hating! By getting angry and hating! I want you to show me how to quit. Because if you can teach me how to get some serenity, then, with the treatments I am getting here, I'll be all right."

The pastor was silent for a moment. Then he said, "I see you have a Bible on your table. Do you use it?"

"Oh, I read it. So I guess you could say I use it. But my trouble is that I don't know how to practice what it teaches. You go ahead! You show me how! Read it to me. Give me the works!"

The pastor agreed to this rather unusual request. He outlined a technique for the physician. He asked him to confess all his resentment and hatreds and everything he had done that was wrong, then to ask for forgiveness. "Don't just believe that God is going to forgive you some time or other," he added, "but that he already has done so, even while you ask."

Later, when the doctor was well again and able to leave the hospital, he kept in touch with the minister. He began to go to church regularly. Gradually he learned how to apply his religion in a practical way; he discovered the wisdom of not being self-centered and accepting the fact that something must be left to God. He was happier, and healthier, than he had ever been.

It is axiomatic that what we think and feel has a vital effect on our health. The theory of psychosomatic medicine (*psyche*—mind; *soma*—body) is based on the fact that there is a real connection between our state of mind and the state of our health. Our attitudes, our philosophy of life, our goals, our ethical ideals, all of these are big factors in our physical well-being.

A prominent physician has said that a very high proportion of the illnesses that he sees in his practice is caused by fear, anger, and guilt. These three emotions are the three great enemies of health. And when these emotions are repressed into the unconscious mind, they rankle and fester; they give rise to anxiety and depression. There is no question but that they contribute largely to ailments such as high blood pressure, heart diseases, chronic fatigue, stomach ulcer, and many skin disorders.

The profound influence of incorrect inner attitudes on health was recognized in a statement made at a meeting of the American Medical Association. It said, in part:

"Working hard to achieve fame and prestige, the average American shows many vague illnesses with very acute symptoms. There are an usual number of social climbers or social rushers who complain about stomach ulcers and an overactive thyroid gland. Many patients with nausea are not the victims of tainted food; they 'cannot stomach' a personal or family situation that confronts them.

"Perhaps this situation is caused by an alcoholic husband, a faithless mate, or a broken love affair; whatever it is it produces a deep and pervading discontent. Not a few patients complaining of skin eruptions have no infection; they are letting mental worries 'get under their skin.' Lots of people are sick because the mind tells them to act along certain lines and they fail to act on their moral convictions."

The modern physician thinks of man as a single unit which functions on many different levels. There is the level of chemistry—the digestion of food, for instance. The mechanical level involves movement of various parts of the body, such as the arms and legs. At the physiological level are the glands, the circulation of the blood and so on. And, finally, there is the psychological level, on which the total person operates. These four levels overlap; they cannot be separated from each other.

Long ago medicine was little more than superstition, largely based on what ancient authorities had said. Before it could reach its present comprehensive view, it had to break through the authoritarian attitudes which had dominated it for centuries. Then an era of experimentation began. Physicians discovered new drugs. They discovered the circulation of the blood. And the microscope revealed that the human body is composed of tiny cells.

The long march of experimental, but still materialistic, medicine gathered momentum. At one time it was thought that germs were the cause of almost all sickness. By 1900 the concept of disease, in the minds of most physicians, was about as follows: Disease is caused by changes in the cells of the body brought about primarily by germs, injuries, or by poisons, generated either by the body itself or brought in from the outside.

Since then, psychosomatic medicine has added an all-important new concept: The cells of the body can also be injured by fear, anger, resentment, anxiety, depression and especially by long continued, unabated tension. For example, a group of neurologists at the College of Physicians and Surgeons of Columbia University has concluded, after a thorough study, that many chronic headaches are due chiefly to tension and worry.

So health may well depend on one's outlook toward life, how one feels about what one is doing, or not doing, and how one reacts to other people. How situations at work and at home are handled is important to health. It is frequently influenced by certain emotional patterns formed in childhood. Just what part of the body may be affected will depend, at least to a certain extent, on a person's constitutional make-up. Some people, for instance, may have a weakness of the mucous membrane of the nose or sinuses; others a weakness of the digestive tract, the lungs, the heart, or the circulatory system.

But, more and more, people are finding out that if they want to avoid, or recover from, certain ailments, they may have to change their attitudes and their way of life. They are discovering the healing power that lies in learning what they are really like, and then relating themselves to the universe.

Such was the case of a man who was sent to us by his physician because he was, almost literally, killing himself with overwork. He had recently suffered an attack of coronary thrombosis (heart diseases are at the top of the list of psychosomatic ailments). His doctor had told him that if he did not ease up, his days were numbered. The man was baffled and, naturally, frightened. "I'm scared to keep up the pace I'm hitting," he said despairingly, "and yet I don't know how to ease up! The doctor says I must stop or it will kill me, but I don't know how to stop!"

His heart condition was the result of almost continuous nervous strain. To get at the underlying cause of his tension, and to enable him to relieve it, we had to look back into his life story. We had to find out why he was the way he was.

He was a truly self-made man, who had reached his success in business through much hard work. Born on an impoverished farm in the South, he helped his father in the fields all through childhood. He worked his way through school and college. Later he started his own firm and built it up into an important and prosperous concern. But he tried always to make it a one-man show; it irked him to take advice or help from anyone. Then the crisis was precipitated when he presented a plan for expansion to his board of directors and they turned him down. In his exceptionally tense condition this was more than he could take. It brought on his heart attack.

For a long time he had been neglecting his health. He was flabby from lack of exercise. He smoked too much and drank ten or twelve cups of coffee a day. He followed a killing work schedule, and prided himself on never taking a vacation. Although he was fond of his wife, and had a beautiful home, he never gave himself a chance to enjoy his family life.

His constant overwork and his relentless ambition had become an ingrained part of his character. They were his life goals and he regarded them as praiseworthy beyond criticism. As so many people do, he had long since stopped figuring out what he really wanted out of life.

It was as though there were a tightly wound spring inside him that drove him relentlessly. Like a wound-up toy, he just kept on spinning. What wound this "spring"? Simply this: He had taken his father as his model—perhaps rival would be a better word—and, without quite realizing it, was blindly determined not only to equal but to outstrip him. He had forgotten that his father had been forced to such hard work by dire poverty. And so, even though he was now very well off, he went right on driving himself as though the wolf were howling on his doorstep.

It was made clear to him that he was dominated by an old, childish ambition, or rivalry, that had no relation to his present necessities. Then a clinic pastor told him that he would have to reorganize his whole way of life if he were to avoid recurring heart attacks, and eventually a complete breakdown.

It happened that in his youth he had been a lay preacher. "Perhaps," the pastor said, "in those days you knew more about life than you do now."

"I guess I couldn't have known much less," the man answered ruefully.

"You didn't have as much money as you do now, but you didn't have coronary thrombosis, either, did you! Maybe you should go back to the crossroads, as it were, and see what you've lost, and why. Why not sit down, away from ordinary distractions, and ask yourself quietly just what you are trying to accomplish.

"Then put aside some time out of each week for complete relaxation. This may actually spell the difference between life and death." And to help him do this, the minister outlined for him the kind of Sunday that would really be a day of rest. This was it:

"Get a good sleep Saturday night. On Sunday morning walk to church slowly. Don't get there late, because you won't find a seat. Just because you haven't been going to church lately doesn't mean that others haven't.

"Sit down and say to yourself, 'I'm in the house of God. What's wrong with me is that I haven't been in the house of God for a long time. I've been jumping around like a chicken with its head cut off trying to build up something that I can't possibly take with me. And all I've done is to break down my health. Now I'm in the place of peace.'

"Sit quietly in the pew and think about the peace of God. Don't agitate yourself too much about your sins. Don't go all over them. Just ask the Lord to forgive you for your selfishness, for your self-centeredness, and for any other fault or wrong in you. Tell the Lord you are sorry about this and ask Him how you can be more valuable in life. But don't minimize the fine things you have done, in talking to Him.

"Listen to the hymns; soak up a feeling of faith and trust. Look at the fine people who are there. Study them; look for the real happiness in their faces. And say to yourself that you can get the same feeling. Listen to the sermon. Your preacher may be as smart, or perhaps even smarter, than you are. Learn something!

"Then walk home slowly. Don't do a thing on Sunday afternoon but nap, or talk with your wife. Forget your business. Forget the headlines in your Sunday newspaper. It would be a good thing to read the Bible, but if that's too much for you to start with, read a poem. Pick the smallest one you can find, and the simplest, and read it. Do you remember the lines,

Come read to me some poem,
Some simple and heartfelt lay,
That will soothe these restless feelings
And banish the thoughts of the day . . . ?

"Take a pleasant short walk and go to bed early. And don't listen to the midnight news on the radio, either!"

The pastor smiled. "Think you can do that?"

"I'll try," the man said gratefully. "It sounds interesting. I'll give it a trial."

"Do try it," the pastor said. "Learn to spend one day out of seven in this relaxed way. Keep it up. And when you go back to your doctor, I'm sure he will say that your heart is in better shape, and that your blood pressure is lower."

Some heart conditions, such as coronary thrombosis, are so very closely related to emotional states that we wish to give a similar second example, but differing in the underlying causes.

One day a high-pressure, efficiency-obsessed executive began to have severe pains in his chest and up and down his arm. The next thing he knew he was lying between cool sheets in a hospital bed, and all about him he could hear the soft footsteps of nurses moving around in the semidarkness of his room.

This man had built up a huge manufacturing concern, largely, as he liked to say, with his own two hands. And he really thought that no one had done or could do anything well except himself. Theoretically he delegated authority to others, but, of course, in reality he never did, or if he did he always had to stay around and watch them and make suggestions, so that the job would be done to his idea of perfection. Of course he had taken on a bigger load than he, or anyone else, could carry. And now he found himself, at the age of forty-six, at what appeared to be the end of the road. But, although his body lay quiet between the sheets, his mind was seething. He kept talking to his physician: "What becomes of the business; it will go to pieces with me gone. It is a key industry. If it closes, others will close; hundreds will be thrown out of work; thousands, maybe hundreds of thousands! And why, if this had to happen, did it have to happen to me of all people? I've led a virtuous life, practically an exemplary life! I say it with all modesty," he added. "There are thousands of men that can be spared from this community better than I. What I must know is what is going to happen to the plant!"

His physician was a fairly patient man, so he was amused rather than irritated by the outburst of vanity.

"Well," he said a bit grimly, "in this hospital we are not going to give much thought to that plant. The thing we're worried about is your own physical plant just now, your body. We are going to forget that other plant, and you had better too, or you just won't be around much longer." And he added, to point the moral, "You had better make peace with some of your earthly ambitions or take lessons on the harp! But I advise you to make peace! You'll even have to forego the luxury of getting mad at me for saying this to you."

It was this physician who asked the minister to stop in to greet this patient, when he saw on the patient's case history that he had volunteered the fact that he was a member of the minister's congregation. On the minister's advice, the patient consented to see the psychiatrist, although he was "sure he did not need him."

His story was this. He had been an only child of two charming, intelligent, and devoted parents. Looked at from the outside, it would have been easy to conclude that his childhood was ideally happy. But, with great reluctance, he admitted that it had not been. His mother had been determined that he should always lead his class at school; his father was already looking forward to visiting him when he should be living in the White House. Looking back on it, he saw that he was never really a child, but some sort of a symbol: a chemical that was to turn all of the normal but commonplace world of his parents into glitter.

"Just to show you one little thing symbolic of my life: Every day, when I started to school, my mother made a last-minute inspection of my handkerchief to be certain that it was white as snow. And every night before I went to bed, my father 'heard' my lessons to be sure I was letter perfect." Even the servants, an elderly couple, inspected and trained him. It was all done in the name of love.

But while it hectored and distressed the boy, it also gave him an impression of his importance out of all proportion to the truth. His parents died. He married a pretty young girl who was just a shadow in his life. The old couple still kept house for him.

We began the search for the cause which precipitated the immediate attack of heart trouble, and it proved to be a very simple thing. He had overhead one of his juniors at the plant saying something about him and calling him "the old man." He knew of course that this term was often used as a synonym for "head of the firm," but to him it had a fatal sound! He shut his office door and asked not to be disturbed, and spent two solid hours working himself into a great tantrum about his youthfulness and his importance in the plant, and to the world. As he opened his office door to leave, and he noticed with satisfaction that every head was bent low over every desk, he thought, "I'll show them who is the 'old man' around here! And I'll show them who they can't get along without, too!" And it was at that moment the pain started that shortly had the plant nurses at his side, and that sent him off to the hospital.

To all appearances this was going to be a case in which insight came very slowly if at all. But something in his intelligence was too keen for him to be fooled much longer. He finally grinned ruefully and admitted, "Well I did show them, didn't I? And if death doesn't show me, I guess I'll have to mend my ways."

Eventually we knew his battle was half won, when he said to the pastor, "I believe in God. Why is it that I never realized that God hadn't given me that plant to strut around in and demonstrate my importance? What would happen if I really gave my department heads power and then let them use it? I don't mean: What would happen at the plant? I know that. It would run as well, if not better. But what I mean is: What would happen to me? Wouldn't I run better too?"

One day he greeted the psychiatrist with a grin and said, "Well, doctor, I've decided not to be President of the United States, even if they offer it to me! And you might tell the minister that I've spent the night trying to remember the verse about it being better to conquer one's self than to conquer a kingdom."

The point of that story is not, of course, that hard work and ambition are in themselves dangerous or wrong. Plenty of men and women work at high pressure and accomplish enormous tasks, and stay healthy. But they can do it because their lives are stable and in balance. They know when, and how, to stop, and take time out. They may drive themselves, but never beyond their strength.

Recently a chemical engineer, ill with stomach ulcer, was sent to us by his physicians. Despite his professional success, this man's manner showed that he was very dependent, and a very querulous sort of person.

Over and over he would say, "You've got to do something for me. You've got to do something right away."

And the psychiatrist would explain repeatedly, "You're under treatment by your physician who is doing everything he can to stop your pain. And we're doing everything we can to help. You will have to be patient; you'll have to give us time." But nothing short of a miracle would have satisfied him. His persistent, plaintive demands were kept up in a way that clearly revealed his really infantile personality. Emotionally, he was still a child.

His very marked dependence, we discovered, had this origin. One of seven children, he had never felt that his mother gave him his due share of affection. So he demanded an excessive amount of attention from her in order to allay his fears that he was not loved enough.

As frequently happens in such cases, his anxiety and overdependence became centered on his eating. Being fed the right kind of food was the only convincing proof to him that anyone really loved him. So he married a woman who was especially fond of cooking, in a way similar to his mother's. When he went away from home he always had a very uneasy feeling. And he was sure that he was getting the wrong sort of meals.

What he had done was to perpetuate his former dependence on his mother by shifting it to his wife. In a quite literal sense, he felt that he could not live without her constant attention. But he reacted to this dependence, which he dimly realized was unhealthy, by a frantic unconscious desire to be completely independent of her, and of anyone. So he took on more work and more responsibility until at last he was physically unable to handle it. This conflict between his childish dependence and his unrealistic, driving ambition showed itself in the most intense anxiety.

When people are unduly dependent, and also have a neurotic attitude toward food, anxiety is apt to have a particularly strong effect on the digestive system. By stimulating certain nerves, anxiety gives rise to an abnormal flow of hydrochloric acid in the stomach, and, at the same time, it causes severe muscular tension. This tension and this excessive secretion of acid are then likely to act upon even the slightest injury in the lining of the stomach and so form an ulcer.

The chemical engineer required medical treatment in order to recover. But his cure was speeded up by helping him to reorganize his life along sensible lines. To get well and to stay well, he had to break his neurotic dependence on his wife and learn a more adult relationship to her.

"You can't expect your mother or your wife to live forever, or to be at your side always," the pastor told him. "It's not very wise ever to build too much dependence on flesh and blood. You should have faith in Almighty God, not in frail human nature."

The pastor asked him to think of God as a great mother, a concept that startled him but also comforted him. "As one whom his mother comforteth, so will I comfort you." And in another verse, "They shall hunger 'no more, neither thirst any more." This is like a mother who puts her child to bed at night, covers him up, kisses him good night and whispers to him, "Nothing will hurt you. Do not be afraid."

"Our physical mothers must some day leave us," the minister added, "but God never does. You can put your dependence in Him. He will never be false to you or fail you. God watches over you, 'even as a hen gathereth her chickens under her wings.'"

It was then suggested that he put aside a fifteen-minute period for quietness at the same time each day. Nothing must interfere with it. During that time he must meditate on God as a great, kindly, watchful mother. He was told it would be a good idea for him to find as many passages as he could in the Bible that refer to God's protection, and memorize them. This would literally permeate his mind with the idea of God's protectiveness.

"And in this quiet period you must practice doing nothing," the pastor said. "It is a hard prescription. But you must learn the art of emptying your mind of every thought of your troubles. Let your office and your business and the irritations of the day fade from your mind. Then say to yourself, 'My mind is now being filled with the peace of God.'

"Start back as far as you can to remember and picture all the pleasant memories of your whole life. Let your thoughts rest on them, really rest. Do you remember ever walking in the moonlight and watching the sea wash against the sand? Do you remember when you were unhappy and your mother laid her hand upon your head? The peace of God is all these things rolled into one, and more too."

When this man was able to see that his overwork was a defense against his fear of dependence, when he was able to place his dependence in God, he no longer needed to drive himself so cruelly. He could then lose his feeling of insecurity and develop a normal capacity for relaxation and contentment. He could and did really find the path to peace, and to health.

That important organ, the heart, can teach us a valuable lesson. It beats an average of seventy-two times a minute from birth till death. And yet it rests a total of eight hours a day. This seeming inconsistency is due to the fact that the entire heart does not work at one time. First the upper part works, then the lower part, and then the whole heart rests. The rest period is about one third of its total time.

We call a person relaxed who has learned to relax as he works. Not only does he go at a slower pace, but he also works with an attitude of lessened tension. Henry

Kaiser may certainly be classed as one of the most high-powered business men in the world. Yet he cushions himself against fatigue by taking a relaxed attitude even in the midst of the busiest day. For instance, when an important call comes in, he will pick up the receiver calmly and carry on a conversation quietly, even though he is dealing in matters of the utmost importance. He never raises his voice or gets excited. He just takes it as it comes, big or little. Henry Kaiser is the personification of quiet power.

One whirlwind operator in the entertainment world, knows the secret of taking a breather when tensions start to get him, too. His solution is to take a ride in a horse-drawn cab around Central Park in New York. The musical sound of horse's hoofs on the pavement slowly filter into his subconscious mind. As this happens, tensions and irritations drain out of his body so that by the time the driver lets him out, he is feeling fit again instead of being on the verge of having one.

A friend told us of an experience he had at a business luncheon. He happened to turn to the man sitting next to him and, to make conversation, he said, "Pardon me, but what do you do?"

The man had been sitting quietly eating his lunch, not bothering to talk. He looked up and said casually, "Oh, I work in a steel mill."

"What sort of work do you do?"

"I have a kind of office job."

"You're an executive?"

"Yes, they call me that. As a matter of fact, I'm president of the company." He mentioned the name of his firm. It was a large steel company.

Our friend's curiosity was now more aroused than ever. "Tell me," he said, "what did you do before you were president?"

"I started as a puddler in one of our mills."

"You're a wonderful example of the great American success story! You don't seem to be very excited about it."

"Well," he said calmly, "I'll tell you. I almost put myself in the cemetery getting there."

"What was your first thought after you were made president?"

"My first thought," he said with a slow smile, "was, 'Now I can go fishing without asking anybody's permission.' "

This man, who was famous for his ability to turn out a prodigious amount of work, had learned, out of hard necessity, not to fight his job. He knew that by taking it easy from time to time he would be able to accomplish more and to live longer.

William Jennings Bryan used to undertake political speaking tours that would have killed most men. They certainly wore everybody out who went with him. Frequently he would have to change trains at three or four o'clock in the morning. He was seldom able to take off his clothes and get into bed, but he had the ability to slump down in his seat on the train and fall into a deep, untroubled slumber. Nothing bothered him. He could stand a grueling program of speech after speech without being perturbed.

But it was not only his ability to sleep anywhere that saved him, it was his strong sense of the presence of God that afforded him the capacity to relax, and draw on new strength with which to go ahead with his almost unbelievably strenuous life.

On a certain railroad there is a Pullman conductor who could teach most of us how to avoid damaging tension. One night, through some error, an old-fashioned twelve-section sleeper was substituted for the roomette car on his train. The passengers angrily, but fruitlessly, besieged him with demands for the accommodations they had reserved. He patiently got them to bed in what accommodations he had.

"You've had quite an evening, haven't you!" said one passenger later. "They said some pretty rough things to you. But you don't seem to be upset by it. What is your secret for keeping so calm?"

"It's this," he answered. "I do the best I can and let it go at that! The man who trained me for this work gave me three rules. 'First,' he said, 'work hard; second, be courteous; third, and biggest, put your trust in God.' And with His help I've been able to remain calm in even the hardest situations."

Most people have come to realize that to stay healthy they need a balanced diet; they are vitamin conscious, and they understand that their bodies require a variety of foods. But they are much less likely to be aware that a balanced "diet" of activities, with varied outlets for their emotions, is equally important to their well-being.

A rounded-out program of work and play is just as important in the total health picture as a balanced intake of fats, proteins and carbohydrates. A person has to work to live, naturally. But he also needs some form of recreation: sports, reading, the theater or motion pictures, taking walks, whatever gives him pleasure and takes his mind off his responsibilities. All work and no play make Jack not only a dull boy, but in all likelihood a sick one as well.

But most important of all is the emotional atmosphere in which one lives while he works or plays. Of course one cannot thrive if his world is full of hatred and anger. But it is equally important to realize that there is no thriving in a sort of neutral world of neither hate nor love. It is not enough simply to hate no one. There is a more positive need. It is a basic teaching of psychiatry that we must love or fall ill. Man needs the love and the warmth and the affectionate give and take of true friendship. And, just as a lack of vitamins may, in extreme cases, result in such diseases as scurvy or pellagra, so one who denies himself adequate emotional expression is apt to suffer from what might be called a sort of "psychological scurvy." He surely becomes a victim of chronic fatigue, a weariness of body and mind that no amount of rest will relieve.

A case in point is Joan, a young school teacher who, when she came to us, was a semi-invalid. She was wretchedly tired all of the time. Although she was able to do her class work, as soon as she got home in the afternoon she would go to bed and stay there. Her family physician examined her and found nothing organically wrong. On his advice she took a six months' vacation, but when she returned she felt even more exhausted.

"You've got to help me," she said in great agitation. "I can't stand feeling this way much longer."

Finally she became calm enough to give us the facts about herself. She had two older sisters, both of whom were exceptionally beautiful. As a child she was completely intimidated by their good looks and felt incapable of competing with them on a social level. So she gave up trying. It was as though she had looked at them one day and said to herself, "They're too much for me. I'll let them have the beaux, and the dates, and all the rest of it. But since I'm at least as intelligent as they are, I'll concentrate on that." She put her nose in her books and kept it there for the next twenty years. At school and college her marks were perfect, but her friendships nonexistent.

Unconsciously her early sense of inferiority to her sisters deepened into a conviction that there was no use in trying to establish any lasting social relationships whatsoever. She repressed all her natural feeling of affection and friendship toward women, as well as men. Her life was empty.

She eventually became a teacher and, at the same time, studied for an M.A. degree, and then a Ph.D. Studying and teaching were her only outlets for gaining satisfaction.

But intellectual activities are not enough.

After her confidence had been gained, the clinic counselor said, "No human being can survive a program that consists only of work. You can't exclude friends, love and normal play from your life without suffering. What is left over is not a vacuum, but an anxiety!" Intense anxiety burns up energy at a terrific rate. This produces a similar effect, psychologically, to that produced by shivering, physically; and shivering uses up as much energy in five minutes as several hours of physical labor. It was her anxiety, the result of an emotional starvation, that kept her worn out.

What she had to undertake was a process of re-creation which would revitalize all those parts of her personality, atrophied from long neglect.

As the first step in this process, the counselor asked Joan to endeavor to forget about her sisters, temporarily, and to look in the mirror at herself several times daily, and see that she really was a very attractive person. He suggested that she put her intelligence to work finding the things she could do to make herself even more attractive: clothes that were less prim and severe, hair done in a more becoming way.

She began finally to take a real intellectual interest in improving her appearance, and in gaining self-confidence. Then she was invited to take part in social activities at the church. Care was taken to place her among people of sympathy and understanding. She soon found in herself an unsuspected capacity for friendship and even gaiety. The interest the young people took in her awakened a pleasure in living that was new to her. For the first time, she found happiness in being with other people. And this in turn made her more popular.

The final step in her re-creation was a revivifying of her inner spirit. From the pastor, she learned how to surrender herself into God's hands and to believe that He was filling her with peace, and with boundless strength.

Joan experienced a real transformation. She had been starved for this inflow of re-creative Divine energy, and she absorbed it as the parched ground absorbs rain. She became fairly incandescent! She glowed with what the Quakers call an "inner light," which has outward beauty and brilliance. And she never had to worry about her sisters again, for hers was a charm that could not be rivaled or surpassed. It was a true, spiritual charm that came from within.

One day she said, "You say that I look like a new person. Well I feel like one, too! I'm a living example of the Bible statement, 'He is a new creature.' That's exactly what's happened to me!"

Joan's story confirms the truth that a reasonable balance of work and play, and an active feeling of love for one's fellow man, together with an acceptance of the Divine energy, are essential ingredients of a sane, fruitful life. From these flow mental and physical health. Without them, on the other hand, the stage is set for illness.

Even the most skeptical knows that faith in something outside one's self is essential, whatever he calls it. For once faith dies in a person, he begins to draw entirely on his own resources. But the world is too big a place, and its problems are too many, for any human being to deal with it successfully with only his personal strength. It simply is not enough.

He may think he is getting along without God's help, but then suddenly life catches up with him; and the worries and frustrations make demands on his mind and body that he is unable to meet.

There is no security and no peace except that which is rooted deep. There are no successful lives that are not built on faith. Only with faith can any of us hope to live a full life.

There are a few simple rules that a person can follow to advance the chances of mental and physical health. They are based on the shared experience of psychiatry and religion and they have helped many to stay healthy and happy even under pressure.

1. Strike a balance between work, play, and rest.
2. Try to evaluate yourself correctly so that your goals are not beyond your capacities.
3. Having decided on your goals, be sure you are moving toward them.
4. Then, having put your best energy into your efforts, leave the rest of it to God.

Do that and there is no pressure too great to withstand. Do that and you will find that life flows toward you, not away from you, toward power, toward health and toward an end of turmoil.

VI How to treat depression and anxiety

Depression and anxiety are the two great enemies of happiness. Depression may be described as a sense of futility and hopelessness; and anxiety as a gnawing chronic state of apprehension. The victims of depression and of anxiety are amazingly numerous: these two complaints are the two most frequently encountered at the clinic.

The person gripped by these difficulties usually has a constant feeling of sadness; he greets each day with dread of its responsibilities and its experiences. Life for him is dull, flat, pointless!

Many people like this are intelligent, capable of real achievement, and still young. But instead of moving forward each day, confidently and with enthusiasm, they merely exist, sunk in moods ranging from irritability, or mild boredom, to severe agitation and anger, or to actual melancholia. They are prone to blame their difficulties on some external circumstances of their lives, while the truth is that the real cause for these serenity-destroying emotional states does not lie in the outer world but in the inner world of the unconscious mind. These are the maladies of the spirit born of inner conflict, in which the victim scourges himself for every real or for every imagined wrongdoing.

A doctor visiting a veterans' hospital stopped by the bedside of a young soldier. The boy lay staring impassively at the wall, his face expressionless. The left sleeve of his pajama jacket was pinned back over the stump of his arm which had been cut off just above the wrist.

"Lieutenant," the doctor said quietly, "will you tell me how you lost your hand?"

The soldier was silent for a long time. Then, without raising his eyes, he said in a low, bitter voice, "Because I was a dirty, no-good coward. I picked up a grenade and blew off my hand so I could get out of the war."

This was the fantasy of a sick mind. The facts were that a grenade landed close to him and six other men; that he picked it up, intending to hurl it back toward the enemy, and that it exploded in his hand. Actually he had sacrificed himself for his comrades. But he had distorted the meaning of his own act; he had felt compelled to interpret it in terms of the most violent self-criticism. Of course no such accusation as this just comes "out of thin air." But it had its basis not in a fact, *but in a fear*.

This man had always been afraid that he would be a

coward, and, in the split second in which the bomb was in his hand he had thought, "Now if I lose my hand I can quit." His comrades all testified that he could not possibly have thrown it before the explosion occurred; the picking up and the exploding were practically simultaneous. But because he had had the thought and then had failed, he felt that he had done it on purpose.

This was an extreme case of profound depression, but it is a disorder which in a milder form assails many people. Generally the true cause of depression or anxiety is more or less completely hidden. It is baffling and hard to deal with because it often attaches itself to some situation which falsely seems to justify it.

Depression is characterized by self-criticism and a feeling of deep sadness and futility; there may also be a marked anxiety. But another most distressing form of this is a generalized sense of apprehension that is not attached to any specific circumstance. It is just there. A person wakes up in the morning, let us say, with a dark feeling of nameless distress which he then has to justify. So he casts about until he finds something on which to hang it—perhaps a threat to his job, his health, or the state of the world.

Anxiety of this sort takes many forms. One person may be apprehensive about getting heart attacks. Or he may become convinced that there will be a depression; or that he will lose his job; or that the government will tax him out of business; or that his children will fall ill. And, typically enough, these people who worry to an abnormal degree are also apt to be impractical or inefficient about putting an end to the circumstances which they think worry them.

There are, of course, people who channelize their anxiety in one specific direction, such as a fear of infection from all drinking glasses. Gripped by obsessive fears, they often develop rituals to defend themselves from imagined dangers. They may, for example, wash their hands dozens of times a day; or feel impelled to take off their clothes in a certain fixed order; or arrange their desks in an unvarying, precise way; or even avoid stepping on the cracks in the sidewalk. In most cases these people, eventually, seek medical aid.

But we are talking now about the less clearly defined cases, in which for instance a person believes the cause of his anxiety to be in his everyday objective world, whereas what is really troubling him is some submerged emotional turmoil. In psychiatric terms he is projecting emotions aroused by inner conflicts onto the outer world.

To illustrate: The vice-president of a manufacturing concern had won for himself a generous share of material success, but was nonetheless a deep-dyed worrier about the future. He had everything he wanted, except contentment.

When he came to us all his anxiety was concentrated on his handling of a dispute between his firm and a labor union. He was certain that no matter what he did it was all going to turn out badly. The other officers in his company told him to stop fretting and go ahead, that it was all in a day's work. They were confident that he would carry through the negotiations successfully.

But the fact that his colleagues failed to share his doubts and fears was no comfort to him. If anything, this seemed to arouse more and more anxiety. He became tense and short-tempered; his food disagreed with him. Finally, as he put it, he became so unhappy that all he wanted to do was to "jump off a bridge." At the joking suggestion of one of the firm, he came to the clinic.

After explaining the situation to a psychiatrist, he asked, "Now don't you think I'm justified in my fears? If not, then why am I so upset?"

The answer to that question did not lie in this man's present situation but in his remote past. As the psychiatrist talked to him he found that the man's father had been a completely irresponsible sort of person who never made much money and hardly ever stayed at home. His mother had been forced to work for very long hours, in order to support her family, and had had little time for her son. So he never received much expression of love from either his father or mother, although his mother was doubtless devoted to him.

"I remember very well," he said, "the only time in my

whole childhood when I received any real show of affection from my mother. I was about ten years old, and I was crying. My mother came to me and put her arms around me and pulled me close to her. The only time! Only that once!"

This man's trouble was not the labor situation. To his unconscious mind (and in the unconscious, past memories and emotions still retain their original intensity) the union leaders and his fellow officers appeared as unkind, unloving parents who had no sympathy for him. He was frightened for fear of not being immediately accepted by them. In a very profound way his anxiety was that of a small child who, feeling rejected by his parents, reacts first with resentment and rage toward them and then with terror of his own rage.

What seemed to him a dangerous and alarming situation would have appeared to a better-adjusted person as really all in a day's work. But this man kept reliving in his adult life an old childish tragedy, and he was unable to take a normal attitude toward his present problems because his view of them was distorted by a childhood-instilled conflict between feelings of love and fear. Whenever he was frustrated in his dealings with other people, the old conflict, and with it the old fear and rage reaction, was automatically aroused.

There seems always, for these depressed and anxious people, to be a sense of deprivation. It is as though the depressed or the excessively anxious were in a state of perpetual mourning for something precious now irrevocably lost.

What brings about this unhappy state of mind? It may be, and often is, the loss of an ideal, or the failure to realize some youthful dream. When a man is a child, the world appears to him radiant with security and full of promise; in adult life it turns out to be quite different! Or perhaps he has had some goal toward which he struggles until, as it continues to elude him, he loses courage. And as the hope and expectation of making his dreams come true fade out, gloominess envelops him. Or his trouble may arise from the loss of some one person's love, without which life seems unendurable.

A business executive came to the clinic for help because his life had become so utterly without meaning to him that he had just about stopped caring whether he lived or died. He had all the usual symptoms of depression: boredom, listlessness, and a sense of futility. His lack of interest pervaded every sphere of his existence. His friends, he said, brought him no pleasure. His business was a job, and nothing else, and he was cynical and hard. His attitude, in colloquial terms, was "Never give a sucker an even break." He drove as hard a bargain as he could and still keep within the bounds of honesty. He was even indifferent to his wife and children. This man thought he loved no one; he felt that no one loved him.

Without love there is bound to be a sense of insecurity and very little will to go on living. He had what we call a gray veil over his life, a most common form of mild but persistent depression. He was like an old, tired actor moving dispiritedly through his part.

Some time before, he had, on his physician's advice, taken a three months' rest cure in a hospital. He felt no better after it. Then he took a trip to Florida where he swam, went fishing and drove around in his car by himself. None of this did him any good. Then his physician suggested our clinic.

The clinic psychiatrist said to him, "Tell me, you live in the country, what do you do with your leisure time? Do you do any gardening, or golf, for instance?"

"Oh, a little golf every now and then. Just go through the motions."

"Hobbies? Interests?"

"I don't really care about anything, no."

"Your business?"

"It's all routine. I know what to do to keep it going and, frankly, I don't much care whether I lose money or make it."

"Are you religious?"

"No, it leaves me cold! I used to go to Sunday school, and I've been to church, but it doesn't mean a thing. To some people perhaps, not to me."

The story of his childhood was, in certain important respects, an all too common one. Having been left an orphan when he was only six, he was brought up by an aunt who was conscientious but rigid and unaffectionate in her attitude toward him. She sent him to school, gave him the material things he needed. But he never had from her the kind of warm, loving care that sustains the heart of a young child.

He soon set for himself a motto which he had never renounced: "Everyone for himself, and the devil take the hindmost." This had dominated, and spoiled, his whole life.

His problem and its solution might be summed up in three brief points. First, the main reason for his depression was a lack of love in his childhood. Second, the only way to get love from others is to give it to them. And third, since he had never learned how to bestow love on other individuals, he would have to have help in order to learn it now.

We knew that it was useless to tell him he must learn to love people. It was something, however, that he had to be led to do. We asked him to start with trying to discover what other people were like and to begin with a simple affirmation, "I am learning to understand my wife, Anna. And I am learning to understand my children, John and Susan." To help him make this a reality in his life, it was suggested that he take the time and trouble to do things with them that they enjoyed, although he would have to force himself to do so at first. And he was told to write down on a piece of paper all the fine qualities and desirable traits that he could see in them. He was to carry this paper around with him and study it, and add to it from time to time. Whenever he got to thinking and fretting about himself, he was to take out what he had written and reflect on it, instead of on himself.

He took a rather harsh attitude, he admitted, toward the men who were his subordinates in his business. He was told to try to feel a warmer, human relationship toward them, to try to imagine himself in their shoes, until the number of those in whom he had a definite personal interest could be increased. And to further this, we suggested that he write down the name of every person in

his office, and, along with the name, to put down as many
facts as he could uncover about each of them: How many
children? Where did he live? Did he own his own home?
What were his likes and dislikes? What were his hobbies?
He was to do this until he found himself able to think of
them, not just as men sitting behind desks, but as human
beings with human characteristics.

And, as it turned out, this became an absorbing interest
for him. He was an intelligent man and, to make his study
complete, he decided to go and visit his associates in their
homes, casually and as a friend. And as he put together
more and more facts about them, writing it all down care-
fully in a notebook afterward, he would study these
people's histories on his way into the city on the morning
train. He would sit in the train reading over the names,
visualizing the faces and thinking about them.

One day he found himself reflecting, "Bill's a great fellow. It's wonderful how he loves his little boy. That yarn
he told me about making a boat for him was really
touching."

That day, he told us, he suddenly realized that he had
turned the corner. It became a habit for him to think in
this new pattern. In enthusiasm he exclaimed one day,
"Where have I been all my life? Where have I been? I
used to think people were dull, stuffed shirts. How wrong
I was! They're interesting! They're wonderful!" He was
practicing a most effective therapy, that of understanding
others!

Then one day on the commuting train, something one
of the men said brought him up short. "You're a lucky
fellow!" he said. "I've been a bachelor all my life! It must
be wonderful to have a wife and children who look at you
with such obvious devotion!"

The next step in his recovery was a particularly important one. It is essential that people suffering from depression replace their old, sad feeling of futility with a
strong, positive sense of *belonging* to something bigger
than themselves, and of being needed in a definite, specific way by society. It is essential above all for them to
learn that, as the instruments of a Higher Power, they

have been put here on earth with a cause to serve and useful functions to perform.

The best way to sell an idea to a man is to get him to sell it to someone else. So we invited him to join the men's club at the church. We said to him, "Many men are shy and uncertain of themselves, fearful of letting themselves go. Often they appear to be haughty, or uninterested, or above the crowd! They are just trying to conceal a shy nature. We want you to help us to help them. Join the club and serve as a 'greeter.' "

"Me? A greeter?" He was startled, but, in spite of himself, pleased at the suggestion.

"When you go to the church club meeting," we went on, "look for the shy fellows. You can pick them! Usually you can identify them by the hesitant way they approach a group. Attach yourself to one of these men, the one who looks the most shy. Find what interests him. Draw him out."

At first it was a kind of game with him, but a hard one because of his own reticence. Nevertheless, he liked it. Then soon he began to take his new friends to church services "to help them." He forgot about his recently uttered complaint, "Religion leaves me cold," and he formed a different concept of God from the one he had once held. He was able at last to conceive of God as kindly and loving, rather than harsh and punishing. And just as he was learning to love, and be loved by those around him, so he felt loved by God. It was a warm, enriching experience. A feeling of security gradually replaced the old, morbid cynicism. Eventually he gained a measure of confidence in himself and in his future; his depression is vanishing.

Chronic anxiety, with feelings of apprehension, is as destructive to peace of mind as is depression, and it is just about as common. We frequently see men and women who live from morning to night and from day to day and from year to year in an almost never-ending torment of always expecting the worst to happen. The actual circumstances of their lives may be normal and satisfactory yet, typically, they continue to worry, to have a nameless, engulfing sensation that disaster stalks them. They bring to mind the lines of Shakespeare, when he talks about "that perilous stuff which weighs upon the heart." The "perilous stuff" of these unhappy people is fear.

We do not mean, of course, that kind of fear which is a response to some immediate external danger. A person normally handles a threat from the outside world by altering the circumstances if he can, or if he cannot, then by adjusting to it. What we refer to is chronic fear that pushes up from the very depths of a troubled mind.

A woman in her middle fifties sought the help of the clinic because she suffered from an exhausting depression. Life had no attraction for her. In her despairing mood, each day was an ordeal; and to get up each morning was a whole day's work. She told us in a broken voice that she had ruined her husband's life, and that she was an unnatural mother who had neglected her children. She felt unworthy, rejected by God; and she hated herself.

Actually, there was no basis in fact for this harsh judgment of herself. But it was no less real to her.

This was her story. She was born in the South where her father, to whom she was deeply attached, was a country doctor. As a little girl her whole mind was intent with the desire to follow in his footsteps and become a physician. Her father died when she was fifteen and she went to live with her grandmother, who had no sympathy with her ambition. A few years later she married and went to New York with her husband. Sometime after her third child was born she fell into a depression which she had for nearly a year before coming to the clinic.

It became clear that she had never fully recovered from the loss of her father; she still grieved for him. She had never recovered, either, from not fulfilling her wish to become a doctor, which would have identified her with him. In her deeper mind she had never abandoned this goal.

And so because in a sense her husband and children were a barrier to this achievement of her earliest ambition, she resented them. Her primitive anger toward them gave rise, in turn, to such a strong sense of guilt that she became depressed. She was slowly helped to understand that the sense of loss she still felt for her father was able to cause severe mental pain. And at last, after a slow and sympathetic re-education, she was able to say, "It's true that I've had to give up something I wanted from the bottom of my heart. But I suppose that happens to most of us. In my case, something else has taken its place—my family. I can see now that, far from ruining my husband's and my children's lives, I'm actually helping them to become successful people."

"That is right," the psychiatrist said, "there is no need for your self-criticism. The facts simply do not justify it. But your relief from depression cannot be gained by an entirely intellectual approach to these problems. As strong a drive as yours toward medical service must have some expression. When you are just a little bit better we will help you to find some part-time service that will fill this emotional need also." Eventually she found work with the blood bank, an extremely worthwhile medical project carried forward by laymen.

She was a profoundly religious woman and the final step in her recovery came through religious guidance. The pastor said to her: "If you are so depressed, so filled with gloomy thoughts about yourself and your family, you evidently have not realized the loving qualities of God! Perhaps once in a while, in desperation, the thought of God comes into your mind, but that's not enough. Through concentration, you must bring Him from the shadowy edges of your emotional life into its center. You must practice thinking about God. You must begin to practice putting your hope in God, also. And I emphasize the word *practice*."

He quoted to her a passage from the Scriptures, the 42nd Psalm, verse 5, which is surely one of the greatest statements on mental and spiritual health ever written: "Why art thou cast down, O my soul? and why art thou disquieted in me? hope thou in God: for I shall yet praise Him for the help of His countenance."

The minister said that her cure was contained in those words. "They remind us," he said, "first, how profoundly the soul, the very essence of the self, is depressed. We are cast down, and dispirited, and low in mind! Then in the most reassuring way we are told to practice hope in God. We are to begin to practice believing that God can and will help us solve our problems. As a result we have a glimmer of fresh confidence, and if we keep on, eventually we are filled with such radiance that the new health in our mind is revealed on our faces and in our entire personality.

"Hope, in itself, is curative," the pastor continued. "But hope in God gives a new lease on life that shines out and shows itself in one's countenance, and reflects a new spiritual and emotional health. By bringing the thought of God into the forefront of your thinking, you will achieve the creative power of hope."

Then he asked her to start going to church regularly, for merely being in the midst of a vital and enthusiastic congregation is in itself a most powerful therapy for depression; just sitting among a throng of like-minded people who are concentrating on the same spiritual hope makes it easy to accept the knowledge that God's presence is real. One feels the Divine force and something happens to the worshiper that is therapeutic in its results.

The pastor had a final suggestion. He knew that it was in the dark hours of the night, or in the early dawn, that this woman's spirits were at their lowest ebb, and that by the time she got up, the day was already overcast with foreboding and sadness. The pastor proposed that she should combat this directly by affirming to herself as she retired that God is never very far away from any of us, and by repeating these healing words from the Bible, "He giveth His beloved sleep." Then, instead of thinking about her sleeplessness, she was to say with conviction, "I shall sleep quietly all night and wake up refreshed and confident."

The real cause of most depressions lies not in external circumstances but in the unconscious mind. Since some depressions need hospitalization, all cases that come through the clinic are seen by a psychiatrist who first decides whether or not they are suited to this form of treatment.

Recently a group of physicians pooled their case histories in order to get a broad picture of what might be called the "worry habits" of their patients. The records revealed these interesting facts: that 70 per cent of the people they were treating included worry among their complaints; that 40 per cent worried about things in the past; 50 per cent about future problems; and only 10 per cent worried about their present difficulties.

So half of their worry was about things that had not yet happened. Now, naturally, one must do what he can to forstall trouble by planning ahead. But constructive thinking about the future is far different from worry about it; and a sensible person, who really wants to conquer his problems instead of being conquered by them, learns to take them as they come instead of being half defeated by his own worry before the battle even begins.

J. Arthur Rank, the English motion-picture producer, is said to have his own special way of handling this. He decided to do all his worrying on one single day, Wednesday, and he has what he calls his Wednesday Worry Club. When a worry occurs to him on any other day, he writes it down and puts it in a box. And, of course, when he opens the box on Wednesday, he finds that most of the things he was disturbed about have already been settled. The rest, he says, he puts back in the box to take up the following Wednesday! In this way, he is curing himself of the worry habit.

When Jackie Robinson became the first colored player to get into baseball's big leagues, he knew it would not all be smooth sailing. He was worrying about this to Branch Rickey, the owner of the Brooklyn Dodgers and the man who had signed him up.

"It sounds like a dream come true, Mr. Rickey, not only for me but for my race," he said. "But there will be trouble ahead, for you, for me, for my people, and for baseball."

Then, as Robinson tells the story, Rickey rolled the phrase, "trouble ahead," over his lips as though he actually liked the sound! "You know, Jackie," he said, "when I was a small boy I took my first train ride. On the same train there was an old couple, taking their first ride, too. We were going through the Rocky Mountains and the old man, who was sitting by the window, would look forward and then say to his wife, 'Trouble ahead, Ma. We are on a mighty steep grade! We're high up over a precipice now, Ma, and we're gonna run right off.'

"To my boyish ears the noise of the wheels repeated, 'trouble-ahead-trouble-ahead . . .' I never hear train wheels to this day but what I think of that! And then, right after the old man spoke, our train went into a tunnel and the first thing I knew we came out on the other side of the mountain!

"That's the way it is with most troubles ahead in this world, Jackie, if we use the common sense and courage God gave us. But you've got to study the hazards and build wisely."

Rickey was unafraid of what the future might bring because, as he put it, "God is with us in this!"

"I have never forgotten that little story," Robinson says. "It helped me through many of the rough moments I was to face in the future. I signed my contract that day with a humble feeling of great responsibility. I prayed that I would be equal to the task."

Another great athlete, Gene Tunney, the former world's champion heavyweight boxer, says that faith helped him to "knock out" his fears. At a camp in the Adirondacks he was training for his fight with Jack Dempsey. Being human, he wanted to know what the sports writers had to say about the coming bout. Not much of the material printed in the newspapers was favorable to him. Most of the writers predicted that he would get a murderous beating! So in spite of himself, all this began to prey on his mind.

One night he woke up suddenly to find his bed shaking. It was almost as though the room were being rocked by an earthquake. Then it dawned on him that he had been trembling so violently that it was he, himself, actually making that bed shake. He had had a nightmarish vision of himself lying on the canvas, bleeding and finished, and the fear lurking in his mind had set him to quaking in his sleep.

"I got up and took stock of myself," Tunney says. "What could I do about this terror? I could guess the cause. I had been thinking about the fight in the wrong way. I had been reading the newspapers and all they had said was how Tunney would lose. Through the newspapers, I was losing the battle in my own mind."

He would stop reading the papers! He would put an end to destructive thinking! He sat on the edge of his bed and prayed. At that moment he determined that, with God's help, he would build a wall around his mind through which fear could not pass! This was the strategy that led him to victory. Freed from fear, he went ahead to win his title fight with Dempsey.

There is a healing potency in that faith in God which can be expressed in the formula, "My soul is cast down within me: therefore will I remember Thee." Recently a minister connected with our clinic came across a stimulating story of how just that kind of faith can enable a person to rise above even the most shattering personal tragedy. He was on a lecture tour in the Middle West. One night in a small, blizzard-swept Iowa town, he visited a man who was bedridden by an accident that had left him seriously crippled.

As they talked together, the man told the minister how it had happened. Nine years before, while he was on a hunting trip, he had stepped on some rotten planking in a barn and fallen twenty feet to a stone floor. He was hospitalized for months. And, although he won his battle for life, he came out of it paralyzed from the waist down. But this man had a remarkably buoyant attitude. He was one who would not for an instant accept defeat. He had an ingenious bed made in which he could pull himself around the room. And he learned to use a typewriter. Then he started a little business in magazine subscriptions which, without any appeal whatsoever to the sympathies of subscribers, he made into a success.

The minister could not help thinking what a terrible experience it would be to be so suddenly cut down like this, to have to lie in bed for the rest of one's life. And he wondered what he himself would do in the same situation. Finally he expressed this thought because he wanted to know how this crippled man had been able to receive so crushing a blow without giving way to black depression and despair.

The man listened quietly and then he said, "I understand what you are driving at. It was difficult for me to adjust to it, too, and for a while it looked like the end of everything to me.

"But I did get adjusted, and I'll tell you how I did it," he said simply. "When I couldn't find the answer in myself, I just looked up above and talked to the Person up there. Before this He and I had only a nodding acquaintance. But now I really got to know Him. I said 'Lord, I'm very miserable and rebellious,' and the Lord seemed to me to say, 'I understand, and I will help you.'

"And He did. He did. He took my depression away and gave me peace. And, moreover, He filled my heart with happiness. So please don't feel sorry for me. I found my answer." So radiant was his faith that the therapy expressed in the Bible was obvious: he had "hoped" in God and in Him had found "the health of my countenance."

Not long ago one of the authors of this book received a letter testifying in the most dramatic way to the effectiveness of hope in God as a means of gaining fear-dispelling confidence.

It was from a young graduate student in a university who had, he wrote, suffered for many years from a wretched insecurity. He felt that everything was wrong, but he did not know how to do anything about it.

"While I was in college," his letter went on, "fear plagued my every thought. I was an above-average student, but my efficiency was greatly lowered. On my return home for holidays, I seemed to have lost the personality of my younger days, and that caused my parents a great deal of concern.

"In athletics, which I had previously enjoyed and had been fairly proficient in, I found myself barely mediocre. Where I had previously made many friends, I began to make enemies; where I had been sincere, I found myself evasive.

"And I asked myself a thousand questions. Would I get a job when I left college? What would happen if we had a depression? How would my friends feel toward me if I weren't able to "keep up with the Joneses"?

"Then I read your book!* I could see myself in almost every example of nervous tension! I recognized myself trying for years to find happiness and success in my work but hindered by one factor, fear: fear of what people were thinking about me, or fear of the possibility of failing a course, or fear of the prospects of work in the competitive world after graduation.

"And then as the book began to 'soak in,' I realized that what I had been seeking all these years had indeed been the thing closest to me—faith in God. . . .

"With God's help now I am learning to meet my daily problems and overcome my fears. I have experienced an amazing change and outlook on life. I have noticed a great release from tension and a corresponding increase in energy and efficiency. I am interested in my work now, and I'm happy. Even if I never make a million dollars (which seems to be the criterion of a successful life according to many people), I still believe that I will develop something finer, more satisfying and more enduring: a true happiness which only God can give me."

We have suggested many ways in which fears and worries can be successfully attacked. Now let us, in direct fashion, outline a program for fighting those dark, haunting thoughts which take the joy out of living.

1. Accept fully the fact that worry can be a most destructive enemy of the human personality, one of man's greatest plagues.

2. Know that worry can be a habit; and that if it is practiced long enough it becomes a part of one's character. For, as Marcus Aurelius, the Roman philosopher, warns, in his famous *Meditations*, "The soul is dyed the color of its thoughts."

3. To be rid of worries about the past, practice the art of forgetting. Every morning, and every evening, repeat one of the surest aids to mental health, *"Forgetting those things which are behind, and reaching forth unto those things which are before, I press toward the mark."*

4. Practice every day the affirmation of your faith in your future and the world's future. As your affirmation

---

* *A Guide to Confident Living,* by Norman Vincent Peale (New York, Prentice-Hall, Inc., 1948).

of this, use the hymn line, "So long thy power hath blest me, sure it still will lead me on." If you have been watched over in the past by Divine Providence, surely you can count upon the same watchful care in the future.

5. Think frequently of the wise statement by the psychologist, William James: "The essence of genius is to know what to overlook . . ." In other words, learn what to pass by, what to forget.

6. Practice the art of imperturbability. Modern battleships have a heavily insulated silence room where battles are planned and directed. Have a "silence room" in the center of your own mind, where, whatever the stress, you may keep imperturbable while you make your plans.

7. Underscore and commit to memory the passages you can find in the Bible which deal with simple trust, as, for example, "Are not two sparrows sold for a farthing? and one of them shall not fall on the ground without your Father. But the very hairs of your head are all numbered. Fear ye not, therefore, ye are of more value than many sparrows." If He is interested in the sparrows' problems, you may be assured He is interested in yours.

8. Practice trying to empty the mind. Say to yourself, "I am now emptying my mind of all anxiety, fear and insecurity."

9. Then fill the mind, affirming, "God is filling my mind with peace, courage, and contentment."

10. Practice feeling God's presence, with the words, "God is with me now. He is now my constant companion. He will never leave me."

Remember that however much depression and anxiety may seem justified by outward events, they gain their real force through inner conflicts. And the way to get rid of these destructive reactions to the problems of everyday life is to attack them at their roots. First: To undertake, with skilled help if necessary, a searching self-examination into their true causes. Next: To take part in activities that will bring a sense of belonging to the group and having duties toward it. And the final step: To build up an affirmative faith in God which will impart a sense of purpose, and meaning, and direction, to the act of living.

VII   How to have a successful marriage

More than a fifth of all the people who come to the clinic come to seek advice on how to save their marriages from disaster. Once, like all young couples, they walked up the church aisle aflame with a spirit of romance, and filled with hope and faith in their common future. Now they are bewildered and in trouble. The marital bond they so joyfully accepted as a golden strand tying them together in love has become a galling manacle. Viewing their plight against the background of the tragically high divorce rate, one can only conclude, sadly, that marriage must certainly be the most difficult institution ever devised.

But its divine sanction and the fact that society has kept on with it seem to indicate not only how needed it is as an institution, but that it is also truly rewarding if it is managed intelligently.

The purposes that marriage is intended to serve are logical and compelling, and quite clear enough. It is the only satisfactory arrangement for achieving lasting mutual love and companionship between the parents of children. It provides, or at least it should, a stable environment for bearing and bringing up children imbued with the ideals on which our society is founded and has for so long endured.

As a plan for the perpetuation of the race, and for human happiness, marriage is a simple one. But carrying it out does not appear to be so. True, it corresponds to man's most basic needs and aspirations. But, all too often, men and women are prevented by the most deep-seated, powerfully destructive inner impulses from creating this happy design in their lives. Their primitive unconscious strivings make them reject, willy-nilly, the very situation welcomed by their conscious, reasoning minds. They recognize marriage as a partnership based on life goals and ideals in which each has duties, pleasures, desires and needs which the other helps him, or her, to fulfill. But in spite of, or perhaps because of, themselves they find that in practice it often becomes little more than a grueling contest of opposing wills.

The result can be seen in the records of the divorce courts, and of any clinic. Here is a vast, hardly varying account of marriages broken by infidelity, by drinking, by sexual frustration, by quarreling about money and in-laws, and by endless arguments both serious and petty.

Marriages are perhaps often made in heaven, but they are always worked out in the arena of daily life; and the reason that they are not always happy remains a mystery only so long as the forces of the unconscious mind are ignored. Even the very conflicts of marriage are rarely what they appear to be. The quarreling is a sort of unconscious doubletalk and really reflects the conflicts within the person more nearly than it does the existing situation. Primitive infantile desires war with the interests of the marital partner, with one's own better impulses, with concepts of morality.

Marriage, more than any other human relationship, requires compromise. It is a partnership in which individual selfishness has to be surrendered for mutual gain. Marriage has no place for compulsive, uncontrolled self-centeredness on the part of either husband or wife.

Our clinical experience shows that a real understanding of one's deepest motives, together with an honest determination to make a go of things, shared equally by man and wife, can often cure even the most stubborn of marital troubles. But that depends, of course, on whether or not the marriage has been made on any sort of reasonable basis, and if under it there is the support of a real religious faith.

The necessity for a reasonable basis of selection seems so obvious as to be trite. And yet people are so often so amazingly unthinking in the choice of a mate that looking at it from the outside one might actually be excused for believing that thinking about the subject was actually forbidden. If you were to ask the average young couple in advance of marriage if they were intellectually, spiritually, and physically compatible they might even laugh. They would just answer, "We are in love." This does not even insure physical compatibility, although they would most surely assume that it does. And, while the joy of perfect physical union promotes marital happiness, certainly it will not of itself sustain marriage permanently. There must be companionship, mutual understanding, and respect; a sense of equality, and sharing of goals, dreams, and ideals. There are no short-cuts to success in this most complex of human ventures.

This seems obvious enough. Yet people often give this choice of a life partner less consideration than they might expend on picking a summer cottage. People will marry without getting acquainted who would not dream of picking their summer house blindfolded. They seem to believe that their romantic excitement about each other in itself guarantees to carry them along through the years.

A young man violently in love married a girl whose beauty overcame all his native cautiousness. He took it for granted that her character would please him as much as her face and figure; and that her aspirations would be identical with his. On shipboard, honeymoon bound, he shared with her for the first time his dream of their life together. When he got home from work, she would be waiting for him in their apartment with a wonderful little dinner cooked and ready. There would be just the two of them, with no one to disturb their private Eden. Eventually she would be the perfect and adoring mother of his children.

With quiet but implacable firmness she brought him down to earth. As for children, she did not intend to have any. And as for dinner, there would be a choice of a cook, or a restaurant. Before the first week of their marriage had passed, disillusionment stared them both in the face, for she was equally bewildered by his ideals for her as he was at her response. Her great beauty had the unfortunate effect of persuading her that she was outside the usual rules for marriage. It had isolated her from social reality.

The man's ideas were so set and unmodifiable, and the woman's so childish and self-centered, that no compromise was possible, and the marriage broke up. But it need never have been made if they had taken even two or three hours off from discussing the state of their emotions and devoted them to a practical study of what the other desired out of marriage.

Obviously, it is only common sense to reach a thorough understanding of what each person's interests are, and to make certain they are not in conflict, long before the march to the altar. A lack of common interests and ideals spells the death of marriage, whether or not it is formalized by divorce.

But even if in the thrill and overconfidence of courtship this has been neglected, the trouble can still often be mended, if there is a sincere willingness to discuss disagreements in a spirit of mutual respect and compromise. Compromise is the key word in this as in all other relationships.

Irritations and annoyances, though trifling at the beginning, take on major proportions if they are repeated over a long enough time. But the explosive energy created by differences of outlook and opinion can often be harmlessly dissipated if they are faced, not with hostility and recrimination, but with an honest, dispassionate desire to find grounds for compromise.

Mary and Arthur were twenty-five and twenty-eight respectively. They provide a more or less typical example of how young love and devotion can give way to bickering, tension, hopelessness and a hurt desire to break the bond originally regarded as binding "until death do us part." The bliss of two short years ago had turned to bitterness with alarming speed. Their final quarrel, foolish as it may sound, came about because she refused to make a lemon meringue pie for him. It was indeed the kind of pie his mother always made for him on special occasions, and apparently he told his wife this once too often. She packed and left.

Arthur felt disturbed and guilty about the threatened breakup of his marriage. But he insisted it was all his wife's fault and he felt aggrieved and resentful toward her. He insisted that she neglected him. He insisted that she was a bad housekeeper and that their house was never in the apple-pie order that a home should be. But most important of all, he insisted that she failed to give him the meals that he really liked. In short she was no real wife!

Mary, who came to talk things over with us, drew a very different picture of the same circumstances. Her husband, she said angrily, was nothing but a spoiled baby. He expected her to wait on him hand and foot as though she were a servant. When he left for work in the morning he would leave his room, and frequently the whole apartment, a complete shambles. He threw his clothes on the floor, newspapers behind his chair; the bathroom was a sopping wreck, "a white-tiled pigsty."

He was a tyrant about his meals, cranky to the last degree if they were not perfection and served precisely on time. And, she maintained, a French chef would have been unable to satisfy him. She, although she tried, certainly could not. And to cap it all, he was constantly comparing her, unfavorably, to his mother.

There was one thing on which both husband and wife agreed. They had loved each other very dearly when they were first married and despite their present troubles they still did. They wanted desperately to get back what they had lost.

Eventually we concluded, on the basis of all the evidence, that the trouble lay primarily with the husband. Specifically, it was due to the way in which he had been brought up. His mother, who had suffered a great deal of hardship in her own childhood, had determined to keep all conflict and pain from her son. Thus she had kept him in a state of childhood dependence without meaning to, and as a result he had not matured psychologically.

She had accompanied him to school even when he was twelve years old because she was afraid he might be hurt in some accident. If he was bullied by other boys, she protested violently to his teacher. On one occasion she had even gone into the street and defended him physically. She made a great fuss about his meals, making him abnormally aware of the value of a perfectly balanced diet. And she unwittingly encouraged him to be untidy by picking up after him from morning until night.

Needless to say, the attitudes a child develops toward his parents form the emotional patterns which he carries over into adult life.

Arthur, who had been treated in too tender a fashion by his mother, was unable to shake off his old feelings of dependence on her. His marriage was going to pieces mainly because he expected his wife, to whom he had transferred his dependence, to play the role of mother to him. To his unconscious mind she almost literally was his mother. And since this aroused unreal and impossible expectations of her, he was certain to be frustrated, and angry at her.

After long psychiatric work, he began to understand his problem. But it was hard for him to accept it. He both believed and resisted it at the same time.

One day he said, rather irritably, to the pastor, "I know that I haven't any solid reason for not accepting what I've been told. But it makes me mad to be told this whole thing's my fault. Maybe I'm just pigheaded, or stupid. But that's how I feel."

"We don't like to make you uncomfortable," the pastor said, "but if you want to straighten out your relationship with your wife, you've got to get at the roots of what's wrong with it. Although this is painful to you, it's the only way.

"Aren't you primarily upset because of what's been said about your mother? Don't be! You must realize that, according to her lights, she did everything she could for you. It wasn't her fault that she failed to prepare you to enter marriage in a completely grown-up way. Perhaps she didn't even know that it made any difference in your relationship with your wife. You have told us, even, that she hoped you never would marry, you know."

Whether it was pleasant or unpleasant to get insight, Arthur eventually concluded that it would not be as unpleasant as losing his wife. He realized that he was going to have to be absolutely honest and objective about himself, and in time utterly ruthless with his own shortcomings.

"When you feel really able to, go to your wife and tell her that you believe you know what is wrong between the two of you," the pastor said. "Tell her how unjust and how blind you have been. Don't talk about her faults, just bear down heavy on your own. She will see her own for herself. You just go and say you want to make a new start, and I feel sure she will cooperate."

Arthur was warned that, even with insight into one's hidden motives, it is not easy for a person to change himself. He may realize his faults, and what causes them, but he has had them for so long that they have become habitual and automatic. To get over them for all time, he would have to go through a deep emotional change. He would need a lot of spiritual help. If he would sincerely put his problem in the hands of God, and ask Him for the necessary strength, it would come to him.

The pastor talked to the wife, of course, telling her the mechanism of her husband's problem. It was helpful to her to realize that it was not just unkind willfulness on his part but that it was an attitude susceptible to treatment. He explained to her that while she would have to be firm, she would also have to be sympathetic, understanding, and not too demanding, while his attitude was being changed.

The pastor taught them how to apply the techniques of prayer and faith to their common problem. Slowly, but eventually, they created a new life together in which their marriage pattern was completely reshaped.

We have stressed the importance of spiritual, intellectual and sexual compatibility. Men and women must treat each other as husbands and wives rather than as fantasy substitutes for parents, because that is of basic importance to successful marriage.

The Johnsons were a young couple who were about to break up. As the husband put it, "I don't know what's happened to my wife. At first she was a wonderful, loving person. We've only been married a year, and now most of the time she's just plain mean. I can't take it!"

Here was a problem in which both were to blame, although most of the difficulty, we discovered later, actually lay with the wife. The husband felt disappointed in his wife because she fell short of the standard he had set for her, which was based on his mother. The wife, on the other hand, was taking out on her husband an old rage against her father. In a sense they were not living with each other, but with fantasy-memories of their parents, and this of course is no formula for marital bliss.

As it happened, her father had been a strict disciplinarian who applied the tactics of a drill sergeant to his children. He expected them to behave as no normal children could. She remembered one incident which, for her, summed up his whole attitude. One day, when she was about eight, she had come in late for dinner. Her father banged the table. "You're late," he stormed. "What do you mean by being late?"

She was silent. Then suddenly she said, her heart pounding, "Who are you talking to like that?"

Amazed, he shouted, "Leave the table. Go to your room."

She went. She was so angry at her father that she did not even feel hurt. And she never got over her anger. Unconsciously, she regarded his bullying as an utter rejection of herself and her love for him. She grew up filled with hostility, which was largely unconscious, toward all men. Without knowing it, she wanted to punish them all as a revenge for her father's rejection of her. Even her husband was no exception.

But since he himself was somewhat immature in his attitude toward his wife, her hostility, even though she tried to hide it, was too much for him. And he began to feel that their relationship was entirely lacking in any real tenderness.

She finally came to see that her childish anger at her father, while it may have been justified, was now threatening to spoil her adult life. As long as it persisted, she could never be happy with any man. It was a desperate struggle for her to gain self-knowledge. She came in each time with some new grievance against her husband. And when that failed she developed grievances against the pastor and the psychiatrist.

But gradually, with the sympathetic guidance of both of them, she got over her deep-seated resentment of her father. She stopped trying to dominate her husband and became more gentle with him. This helped him in turn to develop a more normal attitude toward her. Through insight into their own, and each other's, behavior, and with a new determination to get along together, they were finally able to save their marriage.

The effective but too often neglected remedy of simply talking things over can cure even that most troublesome of problems that besets so many marriages, money troubles. It is amazing how many couples find themselves in an almost permanent state of disagreement and even of fury over this matter of money.

A stable marriage, with good conditions for rearing children, must be secure, and this security is, very wisely, one of the strongest influences in a woman's selection of a mate. When on the neurotic whim of the husband a woman is denied this sense of security, then there is usually serious trouble in keeping the family intact.

In our society the possession of money is one of the main ways in which security is maintained. And women are often made bitterly resentful by husbands who refuse to take them into full partnership in the problems that revolve around family finances. Many men wreck their marriages in this way with childish abandon. The conditions under which we live require that many women must invest their entire energy in the partnership of marriage. But all too often they are allowed no say in the "policies of the firm," a state of affairs which a man would never tolerate in a business partnership.

We recall a woman who was profoundly distressed about her marriage because her husband would only give her money when she asked for it. "When you want money, I'll give it to you," he would say. Before her marriage she had made her own living and she was used to being able to budget her finances in a provident, thoughtful way. Now she never knew where she stood. She had no idea what she could afford to buy for the house, for herself, or for her children.

It was necessary to make her husband realize that he was treating her like a retarded, irresponsible child before he would give her what she wanted, and was entitled to, a regular monthly sum. When he did so, the bitter conflict in their marriage was healed. She was happy and, although he grumbled at first, so was he.

But it is no longer adequate in the modern tightly knit economic society in which we live that wives should just be "given an allowance." Wives must really be taken into partnership.

Why more people do not thrash out their money problems before they marry continues to be an astonishment to all who have to counsel marriage partners who are about to separate. But for some strange reason it is considered vulgar and grasping to discuss the practical details of everyday life. The status of woman is changing very rapidly today. At her husband's death, for instance, she is not supposed to lean back on a brother or a father, she is supposed to have acquired the training to manage her own affairs.

It comes with great astonishment to men to learn that a fraction under one third of the wage earners of the country are women. And a high percentage of those are the heads of average sized families. The day when young women worked as a bridge between school and marriage is gone. And men who want contented and cooperative wives will, of necessity, take them into full partnership in such a way that they will feel happy and secure in the marital state.

Moreover, man also finds himself in a changing world in today's family. It has come more and more to be realized that leaving the entire handling of the child to the mother is not emotionally healthy. It takes two sexes to rear a successful child in a society in which the two sexes have different social functions. The father's influence is essential. And one cannot influence a child *in absentia.* More and more men are finding that it is not only pleasant but personally rewarding to be with their children and that such association pays in their own sense of fulfillment.

It has been only a few generations in our American life since the father was around the house almost as much as the mother. Business was conducted from the shop just downstairs. The doctor's office was on the corner of the lot. The farmer counted up his assets and liabilities on the dining room table along with the rest of the home work, and stored next year's seed in the pantry. Father was always home for breakfast, dinner (at noon) and supper.

Men must learn, now, some way to restore the companionship, and the informal instruction and training of the young, which has been taken away from them under modern conditions, where business activity is usually detached from home life.

Perhaps of all the social institutions, marriage is in the greatest state of flux and is also the most complex. It is the greatest challenge and also the most rewarding. Wise partners will realize that a good marriage is the man's work, and reward, as well as the woman's. They will make it a truly cooperative partnership and in so doing will overcome many hazards.

It is a common complaint these days that modern society has abridged the family too sharply; that lives are no longer full enough of the warm human relationships that prevailed in former generations. Women with small children, especially, complain that they are confined to their homes with too little adult society. Men complain that the old days of "big and happy families" have gone forever. Well, to an extent, the people that constituted the big and happy families, if such they were, are still here! There are not so many children, to be sure, but there are still cousins, and sisters, and mothers, and fathers, who live in such isolation that they themselves constitute a problem for society.

With intelligence, and an adult effort at adjustment, could the two problems not solve each other? How well does it work out in the question of in-law relationships? The in-law problem is not so much the in-law problem as it is the human problem. Is it not probable that human beings of diversified ages and background might enrich, rather than detract from, the life of the family, if they can bring themselves to behave in an adult way?

Very rarely indeed is it the in-laws that cause in-law trouble. It is usually the reaction of the mate whose blood relation the in-law is. The daughter who has married on a reasonably adult basis, and is developing in a satisfactory manner suddenly "goes home to mother" when her mother or her father comes to live with her, or even comes on a visit. Or the man who has begun to learn that home responsibilities are as much his as his wife's suddenly reverts to a small boy, in the presence of his family.

It is unfortunate that parents seem to have that effect on their grown children. But much more often than people suspect, the older person can be modified. Sometimes the trouble only needs to be pointed out to the parent and the parent modifies himself. And even this is not always necessary. It is not so much irritating as it is funny when an elderly woman talks babytalk to a middle-aged son. But it is very, very sad indeed, and not the slightest bit funny, when the middle-aged son talks babytalk back again.

And if his way of talking babytalk is to revert to leaving his clothes on the floor, or to demanding service and attention out of all proportion, then, of course, that can mean the end of any peaceful relationship between the two women involved.

Very often the parent-in-law does not start the "babytalk" and is as much disturbed by it as is the other marriage partner. Two women once came to the clinic, one in her twenties and one fifty-five. They were the wife and mother of a very personable and intelligent young man with a promising public career.

The two women had brought their in-law trouble to the clinic. About six months earlier the elder woman's husband had died; and since her son and his wife had large quarters and only four in their family, it seemed reasonable for the elder woman to come to live with them, at least for the time it would take her to adjust her life to some new schedule and occupation. The two women, as it happened, had never met until Mrs. R. drove up in her own small car filled with her minor belongings. They liked each other at once, and each felt that here, in spite of the age difference, was a woman with whom she could be friends.

But they had reckoned without the great urge that every man seems to feel to revert to childhood in the presence of his own mother. Suddenly the family agreements went all to pieces. The husband began to leave his linen around like a child, forgetting to turn off the thermostat, and actually refusing to do the chores that he had voluntarily assigned to himself as his share of the household duties. "With two such capable women," he would say, "why should I stir my tired old stumps?"

At any point in their pattern of living where there had previously been friction, he no longer tried to adjust, but in effect came running with short baby steps to his mother lisping, "Mummy takes her baby's side, doesn't she!"

On the surface it seemed an amusing situation. But the trouble went much deeper than the symptoms implied, and the implications were very serious.

Eventually it was a discussion with him of his relationship with his dead father that provided the clue. His father had been a rather reserved man, who had not expressed his affection for his son very easily. And the son had come to resent his mother's marked devotion for his father. Now at last, he unconsciously felt, he had an opportunity to enjoy the childhood that he recalled having grieved for. His conflict was quite marked, and he was fairly conscious of it.

Eventually it was he who suggested that his wife and his mother take the children to the seaside for the summer and leave him to resolve his problem with the assistance of the clinic. By the time of their return in September he had been able to do so.

An interesting point was brought out in his history: Up to the day of his father's death he had been entirely atheistic. And when he had heard of the death he was, as he put it, "thrown into a great confusion" about life after death, and about God. During that summer he became a most earnest student of the "reasons" for faith. And eventually, with guidance but no compulsion, he renewed his belief in a personal God as the all-wise Father, of whose love he could feel certain.

It was from that time, and out of that spiritual experience, that he became capable of analyzing his own relationship to his own family. His reaction toward God had been the same that he had felt toward his own father.

Now with the understanding of one, he could understand and accept the other.

Another case of "in-law" trouble that was about to break up a family came to the attention of the clinic. At the death of a young wife's father, her mother came to make her home with the young family and disrupted it in fairly short order.

It was the young husband, in this case, who brought the two women to us, when each had agreed to put the case frankly before a counselor. It was, as a matter of fact, relatively simple. It was not so much a case of "mother-in-law" as it was of a woman of sixty who had lost her husband and had been uprooted from her home and her friends, and was having serious trouble making an adequate adjustment.

Here was a woman who for many years had activity and responsibility, probably too much of both, and whose life suddenly became one of idleness and depression. It took only a few minutes to make this clear to the two young people, who admitted that they had been so concerned with their own necessities in the matter that they had not considered hers.

There was, in the congregation, a very charming older woman who had just been bereaved of a grandchild and who was herself anxious for some worthwhile activity. To her, as an elder sister, we turned over the forlorn mother-in-law, arranging to have her brought into the church activities on the following day. As she found herself back in the stream of life, her moaning self-pity lessened, and then stopped altogether. She became a worthwhile and desirable addition to the young family that had given her a home.

The urge for sexual fulfillment inherent in all mature human beings, as it is in all other animal life, can seldom be frustrated without serious consequences. Many people, to be sure, sublimate it in ways other than marriage. But in the marriage state the outcome of frustration is apt to be divorce or infidelity or nervous disorder.

Yet rarely, indeed, does divorce settle anything, since the inner conflict which broke up the marriage remains to threaten all other relationships. People contemplating divorce are apt to be more in need of a psychiatrist and a minister, than of a lawyer. As for infidelity, experience shows that it creates more guilt than satisfaction in civilized people.

We recall a young man who fell in love with a charming, agreeable girl and married her. But their happiness soon faded into incessant tension and misery. She had married with a very great desire to have children. She wanted to have a baby the first year of their marriage. He was opposed, on various reasonable grounds. But the actual truth was that he unconsciously feared he would be replaced in her affections by the child, and he wanted no rivals.

His wife was the innocent, and aggrieved, victim of his compulsive needs which neither he nor she understood. Four years went by during which she became depressed and uncooperative. Then he began to feel persecuted, and told himself pityingly that he was not getting the kind of home he deserved.

One day at a party he met a girl and presently embarked on an illicit adventure with her. Soon he was spending more time with her than he was with his wife. But his conscience troubled him so severely that he was unable to get enjoyment out of this illicit affair. At this point he came to us to be rescued from the crosscurrents in his life that were tearing him apart.

In the course of many interviews at the clinic he began to understand that his feeling for the other woman was not based so much on attraction for her, as on the desire to escape from his wife. He resented his wife because she wanted a child to mother rather than himself. She had failed to be a mother to him! He was, of course, asking the impossible of her; and, in the process, he was violating her natural desire and right to have children. He had only considered his own selfish wishes, not ever his wife's normal emotional needs.

"Well let us suppose," the psychiatrist said, "that you do divorce your wife and marry this girl, whom you think you love. Do you imagine that you would be happy with her? That your feeling for her would survive a season or two?"

"I did think so," the man said in a miserable voice, "but now I don't know!"

"Well," the psychiatrist said, "I'll make a prophecy. You would marry her and then you would find exactly the same things wrong with her that you did with your wife! So then you would meet another girl, and have an affair with her, and you'd be in exactly the same difficulty over again. So the most sensible thing for you to do is not to change your wife, but to change yourself."

We cannot build marriage on epigrams and all too many people try. Surely one of the most pernicious of these is that "what you don't know, won't hurt you." As bad and disrupting as infidelity is in a marriage, the lying that accompanies it is fully as disruptive. People should not make promises that they do not intend to keep or that they cannot; but if they think they can and then fail, frankness, as hard as it may be, is less disrupting than the insecurity that comes of living with someone whose word can no longer be trusted. And it may safely be said that no one is a good enough liar to be undetected unless the other party wants to be fooled.

This man's wife, as it turned out much to his astonishment, knew about the other woman; but she really loved him and in spite of everything wanted to try to repair the damage to their marriage. She was willing to forgive him if he were really willing to be true in the future. She realized that it was some morbid impulse that had made him act as he had, and that, with understanding, it was not likely to recur.

They were brought together for an interview and after it had all been talked over, they decided that with help they would try again. He admitted that he had been unkind and unjust to her and he wanted to be forgiven, and she agreed to this. She also agreed never to bring the matter up again, a much harder thing! They promised each other not to allow the subject to become a source of friction between them, but that if it did come up again, in spite of their efforts, they were to come back at once to the clinic.

They were pathetic young things. That afternoon they both wept bitterly, but they went home together, hopeful of their future. And the pastor helped them to rebuild their home on a sound spiritual foundation. We have kept in touch with them. They have two children now and have been happily married for over five years.

People get into the greatest difficulties when they are unable to handle their powerful unconscious strivings. They may, for example, be unable to suppress the urge for constant romantic conquests. They feel an overwhelming need for them and they act on it. They have matured physically but remain emotionally undeveloped. Moved by the promptings of their unconscious minds, they insist, like children, or savages, on the granting of every whim at any cost. The main goals of marriage are love, companionship and children, and the maturing of the person himself. But no one can satisfactorily achieve them if he, or she, is dominated by old, unresolved compulsions.

High on the list of causes of broken marriage are sexual incompatibility, infidelity and, frequently accompanying such failings, heavy drinking. We constantly see husbands and wives who feel a profound love and respect for each other but are unable to enjoy a true sexual union. It is a normal, God-given function in marriage; they are aware of that and yet they reject it.

As their relationship settles down, these people find something even distasteful about sex; they begin to avoid all physical contact more and more, on one pretext or another. They may, then, turn to illicit adventures for the satisfaction they crave but cannot find in marriage. Or they may try to deaden their frustration with alcohol.

Their emotional-sexual development has been stunted, in all probability, in early childhood. Sexual development is so fraught with emotion from infancy on that it can, and does, all too frequently become distorted. A fatal connection between sex and a sense of guilt is apt to become fixed in a person's mind.

A child may, by the circumstance of having neurotic parents, not be permitted to pass on from its excessive attachments to its parents to attachments to other suitable people. And this excessive attachment may linger on stub-

bornly and create a sense of guilt for which it unconsciously fears punishment. Under these circumstances, a
boy remains neurotically attached to the fantasy-image of
his mother; a girl to the image of her father. And forever
after a sense of vague incompleteness and guilt tends to
plague every attempt at sustained fulfillment of physical
love.

To add to their troubles, children develop all sorts of
false ideas about the wickedness of sex, or its dirtiness,
because they are given inadequate or mystifying information. Parents may be too inhibited, or embarrassed, or un-
skilled, or uninformed, to set them straight.

All in all, it is no wonder so many people grow up incapable of true sexual satisfaction within the exacting and
difficult framework of marriage. They are the victims of a
sort of chain reaction by which imperfections of character
are handed down, like an inherited malady, from family
to family. A child raised in a disturbed, insecure, con-
flict-ridden home is generally unable to provide a healthy
atmosphere for his own children. And they, in turn, are
likely to pass on the same old neurotic traits to the next
generation.

The final goal of marriage is, of course, children. But
for many people, the rearing of children proves to be as
difficult to achieve successfully as love and companionship.
Just as their primitive, self-centered impulses cause them
to mistakenly seek satisfaction in extramarital episodes,
which damage their love-relationship, so this self-centeredness makes it hard for them to meet the requirements of
their children. Fairly frequently one of the parents fears
being displaced in the other's affections through the birth
of a child. Or, sometimes, either the husband or the wife
may devote so much love to the child that his, or her, marital partner feels rejected and unhappy.

Even if they are in agreement about having children,
they may, despite their good intentions, find themselves
totally unable to give their children the endless attention
that they may need and demand. To do so calls for a
self-sacrifice which the emotionally immature find impossible. Married life, which has been careless rapture, now
takes on a new, restricting nature. Someone has to feed

the child, care for it physically, and walk the floor with it at night. When no one else is available, the father, and he may get increasingly irritable about this, has to forego that dinner party, or a ride in the car, or an evening at the movies. Each day, month, and year brings more and more parental restrictions.

It has often been said that children keep the home together. Unhappily, the opposite may also be true. In our observation, more than one marriage has gone on the rocks because parents are unwilling to make the sacrifices necessary to the bringing up of their children. Their attempts to evade an equal share of the responsibility put a final and unbearable strain on their relationship.

When, however, there is a real, mature love and sympathy between husband and wife, children add immeasurably to their happiness. Parents with such an attitude toward each other, forged out of unity of heart and purpose, can bring up children who will eventually be capable themselves of truly fruitful marriages.

There are many forces, in ourselves and in the world around us, which tend to break marriages apart. They have to be counteracted by all the strength at society's command. Perhaps the most potent cohesive force in marriage, if it is utilized in a practical way, is religion. A rededication to religious principles, a resurgence of religious belief, is often the vital step in holding together a marriage threatened with disintegration.

A young couple who had grown up together in a small, midwestern town went to live in Washington, D.C. They stayed in Washington throughout the war. They made many friends, most of whom were from a very different background, and had a moral code other than their own.

Soon, in the excitement of those days, their life was moving at a faster and faster pace. They both followed the line of least resistance, which meant a good deal of drinking and flirting. Eventually, each of them had a series of brief, casual affairs. They never stopped to decide whether they liked all this, or to consider what it was doing to their marriage. They just plunged ahead, not so much because they liked it as because it seemed to be "the thing to do," in the disintegrating moral structure of war-time.

When they moved to New York after the war, so did many of their new friends, and the same unhappy way of life continued. The wife came to our clinic one day, in desperation. She knew, she said, that if they went on any longer as they were going, their marriage would be completely finished.

"This isn't what I wanted out of my marriage with Bill," she told the minister. "I don't like what we've been doing, and I simply loathe myself for my part in it! I'm sick of this, and I'm pretty sure Bill is too."

"Well, in the first place," the minister said, "I think you ought to shelve those friends of yours. Don't you? You want friends that will help you, not drag you down!"

"But we have to have some friends," she answered. "Do you think there are any other people in a city like this that want to live the way I'd like to? And if there are, where in the world would we meet them?"

"I know the answer to that one," the minister said. "Right here in this church. The size of the town doesn't change human nature. You'll find people in this church, plenty of them, with ideals just as high as yours ever were! And they are happy and attractive people, too."

She looked dubious. "What do they do for entertainment? That doesn't sound fast enough for Bill! He's got some pretty fancy ideas these days. I'd like it, I think, but I'm pretty sure he wouldn't."

"Why don't you let Bill decide that?"

To her surprise Bill accepted the idea eagerly. They came to one social gathering in the church, and then to another, and then to a third. On New Year's Eve, instead of going to a night-club, they went to a party at the church; and, much to their astonishment, found several hundred gay, effervescent, released young people.

There was no drinking, to be sure. There was no need for that. They were sufficiently stimulated by an exhilarating joy in life.

Later Bill said to the minister, "What do these people have that makes them so independent of outside stimulation?"

The pastor's answer was, "Religion. You must learn," he added, "to think of your marriage as a spiritual relationship, the union under God of two loyal hearts. Build your home on a spiritual foundation and realize the importance of family prayer and churchgoing." There is a saying that Christianity is not taught but caught. That is what happened to this young couple; and it was then, and only then, that their marriage became what they had always wanted it to be.

Men and women who embark on marriage owe it to themselves, and to their children who will eventually continue the institution, to try with all their strength to build and maintain a serene, loving atmosphere in their home. We would like to offer these practical suggestions as to how it may be done.

1. Before you marry be sure that you know that your minds as well as your hearts are attuned to each other. There must be at the start a community of beliefs, and attitudes, and goals. But minimize, rather than make an issue of, any lack of agreement you may find after marriage.

2. Grow along together, as the circumstances of your life bring new viewpoints and interests. Do not allow one of you to stand still, while the other marches ahead.

3. Never forget that marriage is not a contest of wills but an equal partnership in which each must share and share alike the rewards as well as the sorrows.

4. Learn the wisdom of talking things over together frankly. One of the great philosophers said, "There is no hurt that cannot be cured by quiet talking." Discuss your problems and grievances without rancor, and with a will to adjust them. But if you do quarrel remember the old admonition to settle it before you go to sleep.

5. Do not be timid about discussing money. It is joint property after marriage. Reach a clear understanding about finances, so that both of you will know where you stand. Keep it an open subject just as any other partners in any other business enterprise would.

6. Do not expect of your spouse what he or she should not by right be expected to give. Your wife cannot be a mother to you, nor your husband a father.

7. Loyalty is priceless. Never discuss your mate with family or friend.

8. Treat your children, not as copies or extensions of yourself, but as individuals with personalities of their own. Help them to develop. If there is disagreement or uncertainty about their training, seek the advice of a psychiatrist or a psychologist, or your pastor. But avoid bickering in front of them in discussing their problems, or arguing about how they should be brought up.

9. Surround yourself, as far as possible, with friends who have ideals similar to yours and who believe in the same things.

10. Regard marriage as something to be entered into and kept. The determination to make it work is of the utmost importance. Its success may depend on this attitude.

It is true that marriage is difficult. There is no purpose in trying to deny a fact which experience so clearly proves. But experience also shows that its difficulties can be met, its promised high rewards can be won. Husbands and wives can live happily together and bring up children who will develop into contented and useful people. They can and they will if they base their union on a true understanding of themselves and each other, and on a sincere practice of the principles of their religion. But the solemn Biblical warning is sound: "Except the Lord build the house, they labour in vain that build it."

VIII   *A solution for problem drinking*

At the clinic we do not, as a usual thing, receive telephone calls from the police. But this particular morning we did. It was one for a staff psychiatrist, and when he answered, he found himself talking to the desk sergeant at the precinct station house on the west side of town.

"There's a fellow locked up here who claims you know him," the sergeant said. "If you do, and you want to be responsible for him, you can take him away. We don't want him."

And certainly James Brown, as he emerged from the cell where he had spent the night, had never been more in need of a psychiatrist's care. He was in a battered state, mentally and physically. His hands shook. He was wearing a torn dinner jacket; his white shirt was rumpled and dirty, the collar and tie missing. His pale face was filthy; his forehead was covered with a huge, purplish bruise. His eyes were red; his voice was hoarse and trembling.

James Brown was thirty-eight. He was one of New York's top lawyers. He had an attractive wife and three children. He had everything to live for, to make life rewarding. And yet he was inflicting on himself the slow death of alcoholism. In the prime of his life, James Brown was a drunk. His wife had just left him, taking the children with her. He was losing his clients, and his finances were in complete disorder. And at last here he was in jail.

This was the end of just one more in a long series of increasingly violent drinking bouts. Now the tide of alcohol had receded, leaving him stranded on the beach of sobriety to face himself trembling, filled with self-loathing, and badly frightened.

"I was ashamed to call anyone else," he said shakily, as he and the psychiatrist left the station house. "I guess, now, I'd better tell you how this happened."

The evening before, Brown explained, he had left a party, during which he had drunk a large number of highballs, after a quarrel with his host. In a truculent, angry mood he wandered across town, ending up in a corner bar and grill in the district appropriately known as Hell's Kitchen. After a few straight whiskies, he began to abuse the bartender; he could not remember why. The bartender threw him out. He came back, full of injured pride and argument, and was thrown out again.

On the sidewalk, this time, a man knocked him down, took his wallet, and ran away. His screams of futile protest brought a crowd and soon afterward a police squad car. The police took him to the station house to keep him from getting into even more serious trouble.

"That's all I can remember," Brown said. "It's enough.

Anything might have happened to me. In my state of mind, I might have done anything."

"You're right," said the psychiatrist. "You might have indeed! So what's next?" He had listened patiently to the details of the past disastrous evening that were not, in themselves, very important, because what mattered was to get the man to talk about the underlying causes that had brought these events about.

"I'm scared! This drinking is the craziest thing I've ever done. I've lot my clients because they cannot count on me any more. My wife has given me up as hopeless. My kids are ashamed of me. And now this! I'm as low as I can get; I just can't get any lower! But I'm through. I'm through drinking once and for all."

The psychiatrist was silent.

"I know," Brown continued, "you've heard this line before. But this time I mean it. Something has happened to me. If you will go on helping me, if you will stick by me, I'll never take another drink as long as I live." Five years have passed since that morning and he still has not broken that promise; and it is our belief that he never will. But his sobriety is not due to "will power"; it is due to understanding and faith.

Unconsciously James Brown drank to try to blot out feelings welling up from his unconscious mind, planted in him in his early childhood, that were too terrible and frightening for him to tolerate. When he was still a very small boy his mother and father had begun an angry, never-ending dispute about his upbringing. His mother wanted him to have a thorough religious training; his father was furiously opposed. And, although they were divorced when he was only eight, they continued to fight about him. Their bitter conflict instilled its counterpart in his own childish mind. But it was a conflict which he was unable to solve, because its complete nature and source were hidden from him.

He was very much attached to both his parents. But to obey one meant to disobey the other. This had made it impossible for him to please them both, of which he was constantly made conscious. And so, out of despair and frustration and anger, he came to hate both of them, with an equal intensity. He was not aware of the full strength of his hatred, but it operated in him powerfully, smoldering and flaring up like an underground fire. He drank, it might just be said, to put out the fire of this hatred, which was just as foolish and just as futile as attempting to douse a blaze with gasoline.

At first he drank only infrequently, and not very much at a time. But the frequency and the amount increased until, once he had started to drink, he could not stop until he was thoroughly drunk. Eventually he discovered, to his despair, what it was like to need a stiff drink before breakfast, so that the day could be endured! The "cure" that he was attempting for his emotional illness was, of course, no cure at all. Actually, it increased it. And neither will power nor good intentions nor firm resolve to mend his ways were, in themselves, enough.

His experience that night had a revolutionary effect on him. It opened his eyes in a way nothing had before. As the saying goes, he had hit bottom. For the first time he really wanted, and could accept, help. He had discovered that the only way he could finally solve his unconscious conflict was not by drowning it in alcohol, but by a thoroughgoing change in himself.

Now he could be guided along the path to a fundamental understanding of his underlying problem and gain real insight into it. Much of his difficulty was his own conflict about religion. And so, at the same time, he was shown the way to a firm trust in a loving, forgiving, and protective God. The result was that he found the strength at last to give up, once and for all, this compulsive drinking.

Heavy drinking like James Brown's is the telltale sign of a tense, uneasy spirit. Today, in our troubled world, such unhappy spirits are legion. Scientifically established estimates reveal that there are, in this country, some 60,-000,000 people who drink now and then, "just to be sociable." They can take it or leave it. But there are 3,750,-000 people who more or less frequently drink until they become drunk. Of them, 750,000 men and women, compulsive drinkers, are so dependent on alcohol, so addicted to it, that they can neither give it up, no matter what it

does to their lives, nor, once they start drinking, stop until
they are close to insensibility. To them drinking has
brought, or will bring, some definite physical or mental
disorder. They are drinking themselves into hospitals or
mental institutions.

These compulsive drinkers are disturbed people who
react in a special way to their inner difficulties, to their
sense of insecurity and their inability to face the demands
of the outer world. Whatever else they may be classed as
(sinners, transgressors against their society's moral code),
they are, above everything, sick people. They have chosen
a deadly, antisocial but fatally destructive method of trying to cure the psychological disorders that ravage them.

They are not necessarily lacking in high principles,
ideals, and the wish to live steady, sober and productive
lives; they are simply unable to do so. They need to be regarded as sick rather than sinning, as patients rather than
transgressors. They require basic therapy, psychiatric and
religious, if they are to recover from their addiction to
drink, a habit which they often detest as wholeheartedly
as their families and friends do.

Alcohol is not, as is often supposed, a stimulant, but a
sedative which deadens immediate anxiety, fear, and depression. It tends to dissolve temporarily a person's self-
critical faculties. It removes his inhibitions for the time
being, and enables him to act on impulse. His behavior
demonstrates this. It has as disastrous an effect as releas-
ing the brakes on a car and so permitting it to careen
madly down a steep hill.

The initial impulse to drink may arise from an intolerable inner conflict. It may be a need, and a desire, to establish the warm, affectionate companionship which seems
out of the question under ordinary circumstances. And
liquor does frequently accomplish this purpose for a short
time. But then, inevitably, the opposite result is achieved.
Since the wildest, most primitive drives of the unconscious
are unleashed, the drunken person usually exhibits the
alarming spectacle of a person gripped by the raw, naked
unconscious strivings which he is able to hold in check
when sober.

Liquor sharpens the very pain it is intended to remove.

And the usual "morning after" brings a frightening, unbearable memory of having committed all sorts of hostile thoughts and acts. The pain of guilt, anxiety and insecurity is worse than ever. Typically, this is a time of self-accusation, shame, terror and resolving never to do it again. Unhappily, these resolutions prove to be only chaff before the tornado of an ever intensified craving for alcohol.

Will power alone, no matter how many anguished appeals are directed to it, is of little help. Since will power is made up not only of the conscious, but also of the unconscious desires, a completely normal person can decide to do something and stick to it; the conscious and unconscious parts of his mind are working together. But not so with someone who is strongly influenced by old, infantile, sick compulsions. He may decide, with desperate resolve, to follow a certain course; but his unconscious mind, opposed to his conscious wishes, undermines his decision.

Therefore, to cure a person of drinking, the very roots of the disease must be destroyed. The whole personality must be treated. And, as in the case of most disorders, the sooner after its onset treatment is given, the more effective it is.

A young girl, pretty and intelligent, only a year out of college, began to drink excessively. Once or twice a week she would just get drunk. The reason she gave herself for this pathological behavior was that she was bored and depressed. There just seemed to be nothing in her life that gave her any pleasure. She drank, she said, because she was too weary of life to endure it.

"How much do you drink? Last night, for instance?"

"Well, last night I had five martinis before dinner and eight scotches after."

"Why? Do you really know why? Why you do it?"

"Oh I felt so awful! I just had to cheer myself up some way or other!"

This young woman lived with her mother and, although they seldom quarreled, there was a great deal of tension between them. Of course, when the girl would come home late, and drunk, her mother would be waiting up to reproach her for her conduct, her "immoral, irresponsible" behavior. Then they would argue and the girl would wake up the next morning feeling guilty and repentant about her drinking and the things she had said to her mother. But a few days later she would do it all over again.

The girl's resentment toward her mother was the real trouble in her life. It was far stronger than even she herself realized. She had been dominated all her life by her. "I just hate living with my mother. I just hate it!" she said. "She is always insisting on my doing this or that, and always criticizing me, and always complaining about the way I live!" Now she wanted to leave her mother and live by herself, but she felt it was her duty to stay at home "because Mother would be left alone." This dilemma kept her in a state of suppressed fury. And the accompanying sense of guilt, which she was aware of as constant depression, aroused a psychic pain which she tried to escape in alcohol, just as a person may take morphine to kill physical pain.

By gaining insight into her resentment toward her mother, she eventually got it under control. The therapy of sound religious faith helped to eradicate the poisonous roots of ill will. Then it became possible for her to modify her way of life. She took a job, which made her economically independent, and moved into an apartment of her own. Under these conditions, she was able to maintain a normal, friendly relationship with her mother. She met a young man and became engaged to him. And she stopped drinking. She could do so now because the underlying cause of it was dissipated.

Even though she was potentially an alcoholic, she had a relatively simple and quick recovery. She was one of the lucky ones. For once drinking has become a settled, long-term habit, it generally requires a pretty heavy shock, and prolonged care, before it can be broken.

This was the case with a man, who, in ten years of getting drunk more and more often, had just about wiped out a business career that he had spent the preceding fifteen years in creating. He was still vice-president of his company, and an important figure in his field, but he had slipped badly. One or two unhappy episodes had landed him in a hospital bed and he had been warned that if he kept on his health would be damaged permanently.

He had never had a drink until he was thirty. But by the time he was forty he was a confirmed alcoholic. Typically enough, he refused to admit it, outwardly. But when he drank so persistently and heavily that his friends became alarmed about him and begged him to come to the clinic, he consented.

In his first interview he said very little about drinking and a great deal about what was wrong with his wife and children. He accused his wife of not being interested in his career, even of impeding it by refusing to help him entertain various people who were important to his success. And his children, he complained, did not show the proper respect for him!

"Well, if you come home drunk, and, I dare say, are abusive to your wife in front of them, how can you expect them to look up to you?" the counselor asked bluntly. "Be honest. Why should they?"

Finally he admitted to the psychiatrist how much he drank and how often. And he had to admit, also, because it was senseless to deny it, that he had an extremely powerful craving for liquor. But that was all, that was all, he said, glossing over its true significance. He fidgeted and looked down.

"Listen," the psychiatrist said, "don't you really know what's wrong with you?"

"What do you mean?"

"You've told me that even though you have tried, you cannot stop drinking for any long period. You go along a few days without it, and then you have to have a drink. And when you start, nothing can stop you. Moderation simply isn't in the picture. Right?"

"Right," he said uncomfortably.

"Don't you realize that you're an alcoholic?"

He would admit everything but this! Like most problem drinkers, he nursed the vain illusion that if he could only, somehow, straighten out the objective things in his life that annoyed and frustrated him, the other people who did not give him a fair deal, he would be able to control his drinking. He would take two or three drinks and stop at that. But, he said slyly, it would be a sign of weakness to swear off drinking forever. It would indeed be a confession that he was a hopeless drunkard; and this he could not face, no matter what the evidence. But he was going to have to find out, sooner than he expected, that an alcoholic has to stop drinking altogether. There are no halfway measures.

The search for the reason why he had become addicted to alcohol had to go back to the beginning of his life. He was an only child. And his father having died when he was six, he had been brought up by his mother, to whom he had been a devoted son, indeed to an excessive degree. He reacted eventually against his overwhelming dependence on her by leaving home when he was sixteen years old. Although he saw her very seldom, and achieved a brilliant success which made him completely independent in every practical way, his excessive attachment to her persisted.

Then, after he had been married for about fifteen years, his mother died. This came as a profound, devastating shock. He could not adjust to it. He began to blame himself for all sorts of neglect and transgressions toward her. Then he became antagonistic to his wife and irritable with his children. Then he began to drink.

It was a long time before he could be brought to see that in his unconscious mind he was still clinging to the childhood image of his mother. His anger against his wife was not based on reality, but on the fact that he was discharging against her anger, now hidden, that he still felt against his mother. In his deepest mind he yearned for his mother's over-protection and excessive love. Now it was gone irrevocably and, without it, he felt so disturbed and insecure that he could not face life unless his senses were deadened with alcohol.

He could see the truth of this analysis, but still he would not admit that he had to stop drinking completely, once and for all. "That's foolish," he said impatiently. "I have to go out with my clients and naturally I have to take a drink or two with them. What would they think of me if I didn't?"

Then one morning an appalling thing happened. He

woke in his own apartment with his pillow and his blanket stained with blood from a deep cut in his hand. All he could remember was leaving his office, having dinner with a business friend and going to a party. The rest, until that moment, was an absolute blank. He had no idea whatsoever how it had happened.

Horrifying fears crept into his mind. Had he been in a fight? Had he perhaps even killed someone? Waves of terror and apprehension swept over him. He was too frightened even to move, to do something to find out the facts, because he dreaded that the truth might be worse than the uncertainty.

His equally frightened wife solved the mystery for him by a few frantic telephone calls. During the past night he had, after he was nearly insensible with drink, fallen into a morbid, self-pitying depression. In a burst of black rage directed against himself he had picked up a highball glass and smashed it against the table with his hand, cutting it deeply. Someone had bandaged it for him and brought him home. It was nothing more serious than that. But it was, fortunately, enough to shake this man to the depths of his soul.

No heavy drinker is likely to admit that he is helpless to quit drink until he has gone through some really soul-shaking experience. One man may hit bottom after a week-long bout on the Bowery. Another can reach it in one night in a Broadway night-club. Another may reach it quietly in his own room. But seemingly, at least in most cases, there has to come a point where the alcoholic does something so alarming to himself that he has to admit he is defeated, that his own resources are not enough for him to get over this disease, that indeed it is a disease, and that he is an alcoholic. At this point, when he admits he needs outside help, he is able for the first time really to accept help.

That frightening period of frantically trying to reconstruct what he had done was what this man needed to make him face himself with absolute honesty, and for the first time. He talked to the pastor in a way he had never talked before. He admitted abjectly that he was a drunk, that he could not control his drinking, that it had him by the throat. Without any reservation there was now no doubt in his mind that he had to stop entirely. He was convinced at last that he must never again take even one drink.

Once he had taken this essential step, the pastor suggested that his final deliverance from drinking depended quite simply on the help of a Higher Power, and on his cooperation with Him. If he would do his best, however poor that best might be, he could count on God doing His part. He was desperately anxious to try. And so a program was devised for him.

First, he was to pray humbly for God's help.

Second, every night he was to thank Him for the help given during that one day.

"Thank Him because He is going to go right on helping you the next day," the pastor told him. "In other words, just ask for spiritual help on a twenty-four-hour plan, one day at a time. Every night, having survived the day with whatever grace you have, thank the Higher Power and ask Him to help you do the same or better tomorrow. Don't live too far ahead. Don't worry about drinking a year from now. Just be concerned about not drinking today. As the old hymn goes, 'I do not ask to see the distant scene. One step is enough for me.' "

At the same time, the clinic made use of another extremely important form of therapy, fellowship. He was brought into association with other people who had been through the same grueling experience but had overcome it. We know that in such fellowship one person derives strength from another. There is power, and security, in sharing responsibility.

Because psychiatric and religious treatment effected a basic change in his personality, there came a basic change in his habits. Through acceptance of the values which only religion could give him, his life took on a new meaning. It had importance, and it had joy. At last he could keep his promise to himself, because there was no need in his new scheme of things for the false sense of security that alcohol had given him. As this is written, three years later, it is possible to report that he had not taken a single drink since then.

Before a confirmed drinker can give up his dependence on alcohol he must, we repeat, undergo a transformation in his unconscious mind. But insight, in the psychiatric sense, is not always necessary, nor even always tolerable to the person. As every psychiatrist knows, there are cases where a social recovery from neurotic behavior occurs without a deep probing of the mind. Nevertheless, some change in the circumstances of the individual must be brought about that will touch and modify his unconscious mind, before his behavior can be changed.

Experience shows that reform is very often brought about through a profound religious experience. There are many well known cases of this. We will add the story of a young woman who had become so addicted to drink that she lost all control over her own life. She neglected her household, her own appearance, her husband, and her small child. She kept bottles of liquor hidden all over her apartment: under the mattress, in her hat boxes, in the clothes hamper, everywhere. As soon as her husband left in the morning she started to drink and did little else until she fell into bed at night.

Her husband argued despairingly with her. He would plead that if she would have faith in God, just a little faith, she could be cured. She refused to listen. A minister from the clinic spent many hours trying to help her realize that prayer and faith could lift her terrible problem from her. It was all futile. Consciously she wanted to stop drinking, but she simply lacked any strength whatsoever to go through with it. And she refused point-blank to talk to a psychiatrist.

Then one afternoon the doorbell rang. When she answered it she found a young woman standing there who said, "I'm Mary Jones. I'm from Alcoholics Anonymous. I..."

The girl tried to slam the door, but the young woman pressed against it and managed to keep it from closing.

"I know how you feel," she said gently, "but your husband has asked me to take you to an AA meeting, and I'm going to do it. Tonight. I can't take you by force, but I'm going to stay right here until you agree to go."

And the young woman stayed! She talked with sympathy and understanding. She, herself, had once been a heavy drinker, and slowly a bond of friendship was established between them, despite the girl's initial resistance to her appeal. She explained what Alcoholics Anonymous was and what it could do for her.

"If you will go with me tonight," she said, "you will be cured. I tell you, you will! You will get over this tragic defeat. Won't you believe that?"

The girl was silent for a long time. Then she said painfully, almost in a whisper, "Yes. I do believe it."

"Then I'll be back for you at eight o'clock to take you to our meeting. You will be cured, tonight."

When she was alone again, the girl went to a mirror and stared at herself. She looked at her stringy, unkempt hair, her untidy dressing gown, her pale, exhausted, puffy face. Then she sat down and tried to think about how all of this had happened to her. She remembered what her husband and the pastor had said to her about faith in God. She thought about what the young woman had told her. Then she said to herself, wonderingly, "Yes. Tonight I'm going with her. It is curious, but, deep within me I feel this nightmare is over and finished! I can be cured. Mary Jones was, and I can be also, just as she said I would."

All of a sudden the room seemed to her to be filled with light. She herself seemed to be filled with radiant light. She felt warmth and light inside of her. She felt a Presence. She believed then, and still believes, that this was the presence of God. She did go to the AA meeting that night, but she was not cured there; it had happened at that very moment of illumination, of spiritual experience in her own home!

She became one of the most active members of Alcoholics Anonymous, and in the years that have passed she has neither taken nor desired a drink. What happened? At the point where she was alone with her despair, she went through the spiritual experience of conversion. Her mind reached up and found God. And by making an emotional transference to a Higher Power, she stilled the old ache of depression and neurotic conflict. Active now in the church, it is to her the pastor turns to help other women through the same battle, and she knows how to point the way.

When this takes place there is a real cure. It is this simple therapeutic principle of faith in God which is the mainstay of Alcoholics Anonymous, that amazing organization which has carried out the most effective large-scale program ever known of curing alcoholism.

One of its founders is a man who himself fought an incredibly savage and terrifying battle against drink. He acquired the habit overseas during World War I. He was a tall, lanky, homespun New Englander, who came to New York in the lush, tempestuous years following the war and became a successful operator in Wall Street. By the time he was ruined in the 1929 crash, he had developed from an occasional drinker to a confirmed alcoholic. He thought nothing of drinking two pint bottles of gin in a day.

Finally he was headed for insanity or death. There seemed to be nothing that could deter him from his wild, tragic course. One day he was visited by an old friend who had recovered from alcoholism through a spiritual regeneration. He was urged by this friend to try it himself. It was simple, he said: Confess his faults, make restitution to any whom he may have injured, and turn to God for relief from this sickness which was of the spirit.

He rejected the suggestion at first because he had for many years been an agnostic. But, finally, fully realizing his hopeless condition, alone and utterly afraid in a hospital room, he said to himself, "At last I'm ready to try anything." And then, with little hope and practically no faith at all, but desperately and with deep desire, he cried out, "If there is a God, will He show Himself?"

This was the beginning of Alcoholics Anonymous. For God did answer. And fourteen years later that same man was able to write of the organization he had helped to found:

Sixty thousand alcoholics, the men and women members of AA, have found release from their fatal compulsion to drink. Each month two thousand more set foot on the AA highroad to freedom from obsession, an obsession so subtly powerful that once engulfed, few alcoholics down the centuries have ever survived. We alcoholics have always been the despair of society, and as our lives become totally unmanageable, we despair of ourselves. Obsession is the word for it.

Now, largely through AA, this impossible soul sickness is being banished. Each recovered alcoholic carries his tale to the next. In a brief fourteen years the AA has spread, chain-letter fashion, over the United States, Canada, and a dozen foreign lands. Obsession is being exorcised wholesale.

This message which has the power to bring sanity to alcoholics and enable them to live sober, happy and useful lives is summed up in these famous twelve steps of the AA recovery program:

1. We admitted we were powerless over alcohol, that our lives had become unmanageable.

2. Came to believe that a Power greater than ourselves could restore us to sanity.

3. Made a decision to turn our will and our lives over to the care of God *as we understood Him.*

4. Made a searching and fearless moral inventory of ourselves.

5. Admitted to God, to ourselves, and to other human beings, the exact nature of our wrongs.

6. Were entirely ready to have God remove all these defects of character.

7. Humbly asked Him to remove our shortcomings.

8. Made a list of all persons we had harmed, and became willing to make amends to them all.

9. Made direct amends to such people wherever possible, except when to do so would injure them or others.

10. Continued to take personal inventory and when we were wrong promptly admitted it.

11. We sought through prayer and meditation to improve our conscious contact with God *as we understood Him,* praying only for knowledge of His will for us and the power to carry it out.

12. Having had a spiritual awakening as the result of these steps we tried to carry this message to alcoholics and to practice these principles in all our affairs.

These twelve steps have become a way of life for thousands upon thousands of former alcoholics gathered in over fifteen hundred groups that touch nearly every community in the land. The members of this clinic are convinced that many, many men and women have found their way back to a normal life through this simple but powerful program.

One, for example, was a doctor in a southern city who wiped out a magnificent career with drink. He drank so heavily that while he was still a young man he had to be placed in a mental hospital. After he was discharged from this hospital, he went to New York, where the clinic brought him in touch with AA. Within a year he was able to resume his practice. Not long afterward, he was invited to appear as a lecturer and honored guest at the very institution to which he had been committed.

Another was a prominent business man in a New England town who went in a couple of years from social drinking to sprees lasting for days. Once popular and respected, he finally was regarded by his friends as an irresponsible, hopeless drunk. People avoided him, and his business fell away to nothing. He was really down and out. A friend took him to Alcoholics Anonymous and there he had a healing spiritual experience. In a short time he regained his position as one of the most popular and successful men in his community.

We could detail such cases almost endlessly. We know from them that the twelve steps of AA can lead any alcoholic, who earnestly and sincerely follows them, out of despair and into a greater happiness than he has ever before enjoyed. But the twelve first stumbling steps must be guided by a friendly and sympathetic hand; the element of friendly association is an essential part of it.

At their meetings, there are no formal appurtenances of religion, no hymn books, no crosses, no stained-glass windows, no incense. The room is more likely to be filled with tobacco smoke. Nevertheless, the air is surcharged with that indefinable thing which can be recognized as the presence of God. Present there may be Protestants, Catholics, Jews, white people and black, every race and every religion, all meeting as brothers. They have been brought back from the gutter, many of them from the brink of the grave, to be transformed and released. They have been reborn, in the true religious sense of the word.

The average AA is a delightful, attractive person, someone you love to be with. He is not smugly pious, for he knows too well the everlasting danger that lurks within him and the miracle of his transformation. He is humble. He was defeated and he has never forgotten it; he was reborn and he has never forgotten that either.

He was saved a day at a time. He believes absolutely that the Lord can repeat this miracle every day; it is new each morning and fresh each evening.

Although there has been a certain amount of antagonism between AA and psychiatrists in the past, it is being overcome. Each has felt impatient and distrustful of the other's methods. But psychiatrists are finding that in the treatment of alcoholism they cannot afford to overlook the proved value of AA. Their science alone provides at best a long-drawn-out and often expensive course of treatment. There are simply not enough trained psychiatrists to meet the tremendous challenge of alcoholism. An alliance between psychiatry and AA is logical and necessary, as more and more psychiatrists are discovering.

For example, a psychiatrist, in describing the therapy given to alcoholics in a midwestern Veterans Administration Hospital, reports:

"Alcoholics Anonymous has come to be a mainstay of our treatment program for the majority of patients. It may be said that our basic technique consists of giving the individual patient superficial psychological insight into his drinking problem and acquainting him with the Twelve Steps of Alcoholics Anonymous. We attempt to remove alcoholism, the symptom, from the patient and in exchange give him psychological insight along with the Twelve Steps toward better adjustment."

This of course is, in essence, the same method, a union of psychiatry and religion, which has been used for over a decade at our church clinic. We believe that we have demonstrated the effectiveness of the union of psychiatry and religion in treating not only alcoholism but many other personality disorders, alcoholism being only one of them, which arise from conflicts in the unconscious mind.

Drinking to excess is the most bitter, fruitless and destructive means a human being can take to ease the pain of psychic tension. Even if it be sometimes hard to do so, we must bear in mind that the alcoholic is sick, not merely willful. The reason he does not stop drinking is because with his own strength alone he cannot do it. Aggrieved by the real and terrible harm he does himself and others, it is easy enough to lose patience with him and to condemn him harshly. It will do no good. He needs faith, and he needs treatment; he does not need emotional exhortations, and he does not need scoldings.

At such moments, when we are tempted to turn self-righteous preachments upon him, it might be wise for us to give some thought to the motto which is exhibited in large letters at nearly every AA meeting—

THERE, BUT FOR THE GRACE OF GOD . . .

IX Comfort and understanding for the bereaved

The most shattering experience that can befall the human spirit is the death of a loved one. The bereaved person wanders across a desolate plain from which, it seems to him, every familiar, guiding landmark has been obliterated. His loss seems so final and absolute that, no matter how well adjusted he may be, for the time being it is almost too much to bear.

No theory or formula can deaden the immediate, overwhelming pain of bereavement. But there are ways for meeting grief's first savage onslaught; there are practical means whereby it can be lived through with maximum fortitude. A great philosopher once wrote: "To endure life remains, when all is said, the first duty of all living beings . . ." And in the first terrible period the mere endurance of it seems an intolerable burden.

There is, also, an old saying that one who desires peace must prepare for war and it can be paraphrased to say that in order to endure life one must be prepared for death. That, in a sense, is the thesis of this chapter; it is a suggestion of the kind of long-range strategy whereby one can best arm himself against the "slings and arrows of outrageous fortune."

It is to those who have blinded themselves to its inevitability that death comes as the most cruel blow. Then, when it strikes, they are defenseless against its hammer. But since death is to be expected, then to face it resolutely we need, all of us, a philosophy which declares firmly that we will fear it neither for ourselves nor for our loved ones. As Shakespeare has said, "We must go hence, even as we came hither. All is ripeness." And Socrates said, "No evil can happen to a good man, either in life or after death."

The cornerstone of such a philosophy is belief, faith if you will, in personal immortality, in eternal life. For with such convictions, death can be regarded not as a frightening eventuality but as a natural part of the whole life process.

This philosophy enables people to gain great victories over that harshest of all realities. Not long ago a prominent New York physician, Dr. William Seaman Bainbridge, lay ill with a malady his science could not cure. He was a big, aggressive man, strong and with boundless energy. But now death was close at hand. He waited for it with complete calmness. Only a few years before he had expressed his personal credo in these words:

"I believe that entity, personality, memory and love pass to the other side and I accept the promise that we shall be satisfied. The beginning of life is the greatest of all miracles. We cannot create life. We can propagate it. prolong it or destroy it. Yet it is still a mystery and no real definition of it can be given. All we know is the sum of the phenomena of what we call living.

"If this is true in the earthly world, why should we expect to know more about the eternal? The finite mind has limitations; surely the infinite mind will be able to see vastly more. Consequently faith, as defined for us in the inspired Book, is the substance of things hoped for, the evidence of things not seen.

"As we grow in mental and emotional power, we receive added capacity to comprehend what but yesterday was beyond us. No one in this world can fathom all things. For that greater knowledge, we must wait until we reach the life beyond."

That time, as the physician realized, was for him now at hand. And his faith, so eloquently stated, held firm in his last hours.

It was shared by his wife, who maintained an attitude of serene dignity and courage despite her profound suffering over her husband's impending death. The faith they held in common sustained them both in this heartbreaking moment. Neither of them mentioned what was imminent until the day before he died. Then he said to her, "I might not get well." She replied, "O that I might go with you on this last journey as I have on so many of the others! If you now get over to the other country ahead of me, wait around for me, will you?" Then, raising his weakened right hand with surprising strength, he brought it down gently on her head saying, "I'll be there!"

The doctor smiled up at her. "Yes," he said, "we have had many happy times together."

Then she said calmly, "Now you're going to take a journey to a country you have never seen before. You're going to land on that shore and your mother and father will be there. So will my parents. They will all be waiting for you. When you get there, it won't be very long until I follow, because time is different where you're going. Stay at the landing place and wait for me, won't you? There we will have another wonderful meeting."

His voice had been very weak, because he was beginning to drift off. But when she said that, he was his old self for an instant. With his voice at full strength, he said, "I'll be waiting for you. I'll be there."

In a few hours he died. He was a great scientist and a great physician. That was his confident philosophy. He never questioned it to be the very end. And neither did his wife. She has not the slightest doubt that when she arrives "on that shore" he will be there as he said he would.

Religion, with its promise of eternal life, has always dealt with the problem of bereavement. Over the long years, the pastor has accumulated vast practical experience in handling this somber trial. It is to him that people have turned first for comfort, advice and hope. It is he who holds out to them those courage-giving, immortal words of St. Paul, "O death, where is thy sting? O grave, where is thy victory?" which Carl Sandburg has called, "that cry from the ramparts of the unconquerable."

In recent times, psychiatry has added a considerable amount of new, and highly valuable, knowledge to the dynamics of grief and sorrowing over death. Working together with religion it has been able to strengthen and broaden its time-tested techniques of helping people become adjusted to this most painful situation.

The unconscious mind plays a significant part in sorrow, as indeed it does in all human experience. So, very often, it is necessary, through psychiatry's specialized methods, to examine a person's unconscious feelings and attitudes in order to alleviate his suffering.

Under any circumstances, when two people have loved each other dearly, satisfied each other's needs, created happiness together, death brings a profound and actual loss. There can be no gainsaying this, or minimizing its serious effect. The loved one is no longer in the house, no longer eats at the table, the old-time fellowship is disrupted. One longs for "the touch of a vanish'd hand, and the sound of a voice that is still!" In the first crushing impact of grief, the world becomes dull and empty, and life unprofitable.

People are often alarmed by the power of their own feelings, and by the physical symptoms that accompany them. Their breathing may be difficult, as though their chests were constricted; food may have literally no flavor; and it seems impossible to become interested in anything, or to go on with the old day-by-day tasks. The sense of sheer, utter deprivation is overwhelming.

A bereaved person should, without embarrassment or apprehension, permit himself to give full expression to his feeling of sorrow, in words, thoughts, and in tears, to whatever extent seems natural. There is no virtue in a rigid, protracted stoicism at such times; actually, suppressing natural emotions may result in serious psychic harm. There is a healing force in the free expression of sorrow. The period of mourning is necessary and natural. It is an essential readjustment, while the wounded spirit is recovering from the injury it has received.

However, there are certain circumstances, as psychiatric investigation has shown, which may cause this vital process to be prolonged far beyond its normal course. When this occurs, the difficulty often lies in the fact that there has been something not altogether healthy, psychologically speaking, in the living relationship with the person who has died.

One illustration of this: A young mother, who had an exceptionally bright and pretty child, was devoted to her little girl to the exclusion of all other interests. She took it for granted that she loved her child deeply, and unselfishly, and in a sense she did. But, for a very large part, it was a selfish love. She looked upon her daughter less as another person, with an individuality of her own, than as an edition of herself. This is a commonly observed phenomenon. In her unconscious mind she identified herself with her child. She loved her daughter not for herself alone, but because she was an extension, a reproduction of the mother. The child was a sort of magic mirror in which the mother could see her own image. In other words, in loving her little girl she was loving herself.

When the child became ill and died quite suddenly, the mother was inconsolable. She did not want to go on living. She could not become reconciled to her loss. She could not accept the fact of death and let her child go, even though stern reality, and her own well-being, demanded that she must. She was disheveled, red-eyed, like a caged animal. She remained in this state for days, weeks, and then months. Finally she came to our clinic for help. Only after we were able, through long, patient explanation, to make clear to her the causes of her unconscious feelings toward her child, and to give her a sound spiritual attitude, could she recover from her grieving and take up life again.

This kind of clinging to a person through self-identification, as the result of an emotionally over-close relationship, can cause havoc when the object of such feelings is taken away by death. Sometimes it reveals itself in the most dramatic terms. A fifteen-year-old girl, whose mother had been dead for several years, was deeply attached to her father. He became critically ill. She stopped going to school so that she could be with him constantly. About six months before his death a hemorrhage in the retina of his eyes resulted in blindness. As his death approached, the girl became more and more perturbed. There was no one whom she would let console her, support her, or give her any help.

Her father died. A few days after his funeral she herself went blind. A medical examination showed there was no physical cause for her blindness and, after a long period of readjustment, a clinic psychiatrist was able to help her realize that there was actually nothing wrong with her eyes; but that she was blind because she identified herself with her deeply loved father; and that this was the way her unconscious mind took of staying with him even in death. Eventually her blindness entirely disappeared.

A woman came to us because she was suffering from excruciating headaches which seemed to have no medical explanation. Although she did not connect the event with her headaches, she said during an interview that her mother had died recently after a long illness, and the psychiatrist asked for more details about the mother's death.

The woman found this very difficult to talk about, but finally said that for several months before it happened, her mother had been under the constant care of a trained nurse. She told the psychiatrist, with a great deal of emotion, that she had been convinced that the nurse had alienated her mother's affections.

Then, just before her mother died, she found herself alone with her mother and she knelt down and put her arms around her and asked, "Don't you love me, Mother?"

"Yes. Yes, I love you very much," her mother told her, "more than anyone else in the world." The woman felt greatly reassured by this.

But after her mother finally died she found she could not accept the fact of her death. She set a room apart, as a sort of shrine. Around the room she arranged her mother's pictures, and the needlework at which she had been very proficient. Then she sat quietly in this room day after day.

"Tell me," the psychiatrist asked, "did your mother also have headaches?"

She looked surprised. "Why yes," she said hesitantly. "Yes. You know, Mother had a stroke. She had very severe headaches, very severe!"

Eventually she was helped to see that she was suffering from headaches because she was clinging to her mother, trying still to hold on to her, even to the extent of taking on her physical symptoms. She simply had been unable to face the finality of death. At first the woman was quite agitated by this insight; but a week later she came back to tell the psychiatrist that her headaches were completely gone. She was eventually able to dismantle that shrinelike room and go ahead with her own pursuits.

When our loved ones die, we should not try to hold them to us, bind them with earthbound ties. We should release them into their own new world of beauty, and peace, and happiness. By taking this attitude, instead of clinging irrationally to them, we ease the burden of our grief which may, otherwise, so easily bring about physical or emotional illnesses. We can be sure that it is God's will, and the deceased person's wish, for us to go on with our lives and make the most of our own powers and abilities.

Perhaps a still more common, and even more painful, reason for unnaturally prolonged and intractable mourning, is the feeling of guilt that often accompanies bereavement. Here, again, our past attitudes toward the deceased loved ones are bound to have a decisive effect on the way in which our grief and our sorrow show themselves.

In an earlier chapter we described how it is that people can harbor the most powerful resentment, hatred, even death wishes, toward those whom they love most dearly. This is a distasteful idea, because we feel that our hostility is a denial of our love. And so we are apt to try to hide these feelings from ourselves, to repress them, and act as though they did not exist. The truth is, that hate does not cancel out love, nor love cancel hate. And, strange as it may seem, it is quite possible both to hate and love the same person at the same time. The failure to understand our love and hate mechanisms is often the cause of our later undoing. These conflicting emotions arouse the most painful feelings of guilt, self-loathing, depression, and anxiety. This is so even while the loved one is still alive; and if the person for whom we have felt them should die, the memory of the old resentments becomes excruciating torture.

When parent, or husband, or wife dies, all our past resentments and unkindnesses, even if they have been slight, or have never even been shown, return to plague us. Even at best, we are bound to realize that "we have left undone those things which we ought to have done . . ." We forget that it is the fate of all humans to act in this way and remember, to our sorrow, all the times we were unkind, quick-spoken, selfish. In retrospect, we tend to apply a far more exacting standard to our behavior than we did during his, or her, life.

The sharp word, the unkind thought while the person was alive, was bad enough, but at least could still be remedied. Now those words and thoughts, viewed from the perspective of death, become unbearable. There is no chance to take them back or make amends! And if the anger, even though partially repressed, was powerful, so, in proportion, is the suffering it now causes.

A man who came to the clinic had married a woman considerably younger than he, primarily on the basis of her physical attraction for him. The fact that she was not, in his opinion, particularly intelligent made no difference during his courtship; but after their marriage it became a veritable obsession with him. She was not interested in books, but in bridge. She liked social chitchat, not conversations. Politics, or the theater, world affairs or any other serious subject, was taboo with her. At cocktail parties, of which she was very fond, she was inclined to drink enough to make her talkative; this was very embarrassing to him.

He took to bantering her and complaining jokingly that she was feather-brained. The bantering became bickering and the bickering became quarrels, not serious ones, but sufficiently charged with anger that both of them occasionally said harsh things. But, on the whole, she was a good wife, and he really loved her, and they were fairly happy together. It was neither a perfectly good marriage, nor a perfectly bad one. Then one day she had a heart attack and within a week she was dead.

He was disconsolate. His grief was out of all proportion, for the hurt of his grief burned with the pain of his overwhelming guilt about her. He wanted to die! He wanted to do away with himself! He forgot all the pleasant aspects of their life together and remembered only all the quarrels and misunderstandings, which he now blamed entirely on himself.

And he confessed, in an agony of spirit, that there were even times when, "She made me so mad that I wished she were dead!" His reaction to her living behavior had clearly been beyond the normal. But, even so, it was possible to help him to comprehend his behavior psychologically and aid him to adjust to the realization of what was fact.

In such situations it is essential to make peace with ourselves and to feel forgiven for old failures. It is childish to fear punishment because we lack perfection. We must learn the practical understanding of God's compassion and forgiveness, and that our loved ones also are forgiving in their attitude toward us for whatever wrongs we may have, in reality, done them. We need to accept this reassurance if we are to rid ourselves of the tormenting, morbid sense of guilt that can cause so much needless suffering.

Death seems so final! This is what, for most people, is so hard to endure. A prominent lawyer came to the clinic because, for two long years, he had continued to grieve inconsolably for his wife; he simply could not get over his grief. He was making the mistake of living over each day, in memory, the incidents in which he had been thoughtless or unkind to her.

He gave us enough facts so that we could put together

a picture of his relationship with her. She had been, obviously, a domineering sort of person. She had wanted to plan his life for him, thinking of his comfort and happiness but demanding, at the same time, that he attend upon her even to the point of interfering with his work.

Actually he loved his wife despite his feelings of resentment toward her. And he realized that she had loved him devotedly; that she had, in fact, built her entire existence around him. But his work was of the utmost importance to him. He had been compelled to live in ceaseless conflict between the two drives. When he found himself giving a maximum of attention to his wife and a minimum to his work, he reacted by being surly and quick-tempered. The list of times when he had hurt her deeply was really rather long and formidable.

The clinic counselor explained to this man that his resentment against his wife had undoubtedly gone much deeper than he realized, and that his attitude toward his work was not entirely healthy either.

"We all have a primitive side to our nature," he said, "an inheritance from infancy and childhood. You were revealing this in your excessive interest in your work, as well as in your violent reaction to your wife, just as a child rebels against a parent's authority. She was the soul of kindness to you, but she also dominated you. In many ways, your personality was subservient to hers. You resented this. You were caught in a serious conflict of being pulled asunder by loving, yet hating, at the same time. And you undoubtedly realized, unconsciously of course, that the conflict would only be solved by your wife's dying."

"But didn't I love her?"

"Of course you did. Doubtless she understood, though unconsciously perhaps, your sharp words and unkind actions better than you did, and forgave you for them! Now that your wife is gone, and you are learning to understand the conflict that has disturbed you for so long, practice remembering all the kind things you did instead of the unkind thoughts and actions."

We stressed the necessary first step—to deliberately go about replacing the memories of unkindnesses with the happier ones. It was suggested that he make a conscious effort to recall and list on paper every kind and loving thing he had done for his wife from the day they met until she died: the first time he had bought her a box of candy, or a bunch of flowers; the first time he had told her she was pretty and said endearing words to her. He was to think back to when they had gone to church, or the theater; taken walks together in the country, or pleasure trips; or when he had bought her presents for her birthday—all the memories which recalled happy experiences together.

When he returned to the clinic he showed the pastor a notebook he had filled with all those "small things" which now loomed large to him and became a profound comfort. "Why, I was far better to her than I realized," he said shyly.

Gradually, as his remorse began to fade away, his grief faded, and he adjusted to her death.

A woman whose grief was complicated by a sense of guilt had experienced considerable hostility toward her husband during almost all of her life with him. He was a busy man, self-centered, who often made her feel neglected. They quarreled about this, though there were also other difficulties, and once they actually separated. But, although they came together again, a good deal of strong antagonism remained between them.

One fateful day her husband, absent on a business trip, dropped dead on the street of a heart attack, and her grief at his death was overwhelming.

She had really loved him, even though they had quarreled so much, and she wept, quite literally, every day for months. And, rejecting her friends' offer of sympathy and help, she made pilgrimages to the cemetery and threw herself on her husband's grave, where she lay completely disconsolate.

She had been grieving to this abnormal degree for over a year when she came to the clinic. A psychiatrist talked to her first. He made her see that her prolonged mourning was related to the memory of her hostility toward her husband. It was her feeling that her resentment, which in part took the form of wishes that he were out of the way, was at least partly responsible for his heart attack. And this was more than she could endure.

The pastor was able to make it clear to her that, despite everything, she and her husband had understood each other and had loved one another. Although they had separated, it had not lasted, just because they had not wanted to live apart. Neither of them really meant the harsh things that had been said. It would be an unusual couple, he pointed out, who in fifteen years of marriage never had the occasion nor the spirit to quarrel.

"Let me put it to you this way," the pastor said. "Your husband is now in the vast dignity of the world beyond. When you go up on a high hill and look down you do not see the little things. They are out of your sight. All you see is the big things, the great things. Your husband has gone up on a high hill and is looking down. Those bickerings are the little things! All he sees is the fineness of your character and the greatness of your love. Those are the big things! All the rest is erased, washed out, gone."

He told her that she must have the faith to believe that she would meet him again, and be united in a place where all the imperfections of human life are nonexistent. "You do not need to be forgiven," he said, "because there is nothing to forgive! All the quarrels (and they were superficial surface squalls) are now ended. All the past grievances are now settled. Now all that remains is the love of each of you for the other. That is what you must remember and keep uppermost in your mind."

She found out, eventually, as many others have, that an understanding of the innermost mind, together with the power of faith, can finally conquer even the engulfing sorrow that accompanies death.

Distilled from our common experience, Christianity and psychiatry are here making some suggestions as to how the initial shock of the death of a loved one can be made more bearable; of how the final victory over grief can be gained.

First, let your grief express itself freely. Do not "try to be brave"; do not try to hold it in check, but let it express itself to the full. Do not be alarmed by its intensity; do not regard it as a sign of weakness, nor an uncultured emotionalism. It is a natural reaction to your loss.

Second, do not avoid talking about the person who has died. And it is best not to try to avoid the word death by using such phrases as "passed on," or "gone over"; just say, "died." It helps you to accept it. Make an effort to accept death as a natural event. Recall the happy side of your relationship with your loved one during life.

This little story illustrates what we mean. When her mother died, Mrs. Lowell Thomas asked several of the family's closest friends to the house for a simple service. She wanted them to have another experience of fellowship with her mother just once more before she was taken away for burial.

Her husband, the noted writer and commentator, had written a beautiful tribute to his mother-in-law, which was read aloud by the minister. It told about her life and lots of small details of her girlhood; it told how she and her sister saw the first train, the big iron horse, come to Nebraska; how the little girls even closed their parasols for fear they would frighten it; it told how the Singer Sewing Machine Company had held a beauty contest, the first of its kind, and that she had won it. Her life story was told, with a happy portrayal of the warm, vibrant person she had been.

The sense of loss was deep and poignant to her family and friends. But this simple, human way of thinking of her not as dead, but in the full tide of an eternal life, helped them to become adjusted to their bereavement. It will linger as a tender and beautiful experience for all those who were present.

Third, even in the midst of grief, try, as best you can, to go on with your usual tasks and occupations. The inclination is to stop everything, to just sit and brood. This is a mistake which should be avoided to the greatest possible extent, even against your own strongest wishes. The most sensible thing, very often, is to do some physical work that will relieve the accumulated tension.

During the war, a man was informed that a neighbor's son had been killed, and was asked to bring her the distressing news. He gathered a few friends who went with him to her house. When they arrived they found her on her hands and knees scrubbing the kitchen floor. The man said quietly, "I have something very sad to tell you." Then he paused. "Bill has been killed in France."

The boy's mother hesitated just for a moment, then the brush continued going around and around. Finally she said, "Well, all of you sit down, won't you, please? I'll make you a cup of tea."

They protested, but she insisted. "Please," she said. "I want to make you some tea! I feel like doing it." And she chatted as she boiled the water, brought out some little cakes, arranged the tea things and sat down with her callers.

A long time afterwards, when her time of mourning was over, her neighbor said to her, "I've always admired you for the way you took the news of your boy's death. But I've never been able to understand it."

"Well," she said, "my grandmother once told me that when grief comes, just put your hand to the very next thing that you would naturally be doing. So when my neighbors called, it was natural for me to offer them tea. In that way, I thought, I'd try to keep on going."

As a fourth great step in meeting bereavement, we suggest turning to the Bible. Much comfort can be gained by what might be called a panoramic reading of the Bible, at these times. Read large sections at one sitting: the Psalms, and the New Testament. In other words, get a panoramic view of the pain and suffering of the world and of the victory of faith.

A woman had a lovely daughter of eighteen who went out riding and was thrown from her horse and killed. The mother had seen her ride away with her cheeks radiant and her spirits high; now she saw her brought back with her eyes closed and her face stilled in death. She could not accept it. And she could not recover from the blow.

Deciding to go away to try to forget, she went to a quiet place in the country. But the awful memory went with her. Then as she sat in her room one evening, she took out her Bible and began to read. She read the first

Psalm, then, one by one, read each of them down to the very last word.

She finished and she shut the book. She sat quietly, lost in reflection, then she said to herself, with complete conviction: "The men who wrote those Psalms knew about life! They went through suffering just as I am, and they found the answer. And so have I." And at that moment her old stability returned to her; and she was able to pick up her life again.

When the minister asked her exactly what the reading of the Psalms had done for her, she replied, "They gave me the answer that I was looking for. And I believed it. The God of those Psalms can be trusted." The Bible had given her the panoramic view, the profound, consoling understanding and the meaning of faith.

There is a long-range strategy, too, for meeting bereavement. The heart of this is the counsel that to endure life we must face the fact of death before it comes.

Preparation for this should really begin in childhood. Children are often overprotected from the realization that death can, and must, come to every living thing. They should be taught in their early years, gently and thoughtfully, that death is just as much a part of life as life is itself. It is a duty that we owe, a debt that we must pay.

Training about the inevitability of death is essential if children are to have a realistic attitude toward it, whether it comes while they are still children, or after they have reached adulthood. Avoiding the word and the idea of death in the child's presence, no matter how well intentioned, may do him a serious injury.

A young man came to the clinic and related that when he was only seven his father had been killed in an automobile accident. The boy had been taken quickly away from the house by well-meaning friends. No explanation of what had happened to his father was ever given to him. His mother was so heartbroken that at first she could not endure to talk about her husband; and after a while she foolishly thought that the child had not felt it. So the boy never again heard his father's name mentioned. His father was deleted from the boy's life.

As a result of this lack of knowledge, he had a vague, undefined feeling that there was some disgrace connected with his father's disappearance. But he could neither discover nor imagine any clue to what this might have been. This was the origin of a most disturbing emotional conflict in his later years. It was so deep-seated that it could be resolved only through a long period of psychiatric treatment.

Preparation for death also means that the possibility must be accepted that it may come at any time, and for any one of us, and that we must be ready, intellectually and spiritually, to face it. We cannot allow ourselves to act as though our loved ones are necessarily going to be with us always. We are born into the world alone, with work to do. We should be thankful for companionship as long as we have it. But if our companions die, it is our duty to go on with our work. It is all part of life.

When a family circle is broken, its members are left in a state of loneliness and insecurity, in addition to their grief. So if we are wise, we should avoid allowing parents, husbands, wives, or children to become too entirely dependent on us, or we on them. If this dependence is a source of much unhappiness in life, in death it is cataclysmic.

And finally, we can best prepare for death through the unshakable belief that we shall meet again. The existence of eternal life is not, thus far, susceptible of scientific proof. But, scientifically, it cannot be disproved either. We have to come to believe in it through faith.

John Erskine, a noted author and educator, has phrased his own personal faith in these eloquent words, "I believe—let me say *I know* by personal experience—*that the dead whom we have loved do not leave us, but* in some fashion continue here as faithful companions, sustaining and inspiring us. We find them in familiar places, in the home, in the garden, on the village street. I believe we find them often in occupations which once we shared with them. This constant resurrection of the dead is for me a simple fact, part of my human acquaintance with the daily mystery and beauty of life."

In the heart of every one of us there is a deep faith that life triumphs over death. This faith is a part of the warp and the woof of our human heritage. To the Christian it was best stated by Christ and, appropriately enough, not to the proud nor to the learned, but to a simple woman, an ordinary woman who, having lost her brother, was disconsolate. Her name was Martha. Piteously she told of her loss, and He answered with those marvelous words which have survived the centuries, comforting their millions.

"I am the resurrection and the life: he that believeth in Me, though he were dead, yet shall he live: And whosoever liveth and believeth in Me shall never die."

There is much to substantiate the faith that death does not mean the end of everything, but rather a passing from one aspect of life to another. We have the feeling that when a dearly loved one dies he still lives, although in a category of existence that we cannot penetrate because of our earthly limitations. The line separating this world and the other, while impenetrable, is slight. There are certain moments when we are conscious of the point where the two worlds meet, when we have what has been poetically called, "intimations of immortality."

The late Gordon Johnstone told how he happened to write the words for Geoffrey O'Hara's famous song, "There Is No Death," with its haunting, recurring phrase, "I tell you they have not died."

In 1919, Johnstone was talking to a Canadian colonel whose command had been wiped out in several bloody engagements. At first the colonel felt a complete despair, but then as he made his way through the trenches he began to feel an acute sense of the presence of these departed men. His despair changed to unshakable faith. He could almost see their faces, feel the touch of their hands! He seemed to be enveloped by their presence! And this hard-bitten colonel said to Johnstone, "I tell you they are with us still! I tell you they have not died." And it was this incident that inspired the song.

Faith in a life beyond, which sustained this great soldier as it has so many confronted with death, has been beautifully expressed in a poem by Robert Louis Stevenson:

> *Though he that ever kind and true,*
> *Kept stoutly step by step with you*
> *Your whole long gusty lifetime through*
>   *Be gone awhile before,*
> *Be now a moment gone before,*
> *Yet, doubt not, soon the seasons shall restore*
>   *Your friend to you.*

> *He has but turned a corner—still*
> *He pushes on with right good will,*
> *Thro' mire and marsh, by hough and hill*
>   *That self-same arduous way,—*
> *That self-same upland hopeful way,*
> *That you and he through many a doubtful day*
>   *Attempted still.*

> *He is not dead, this friend—not dead*
> *But in the path we mortals tread,*
> *Got some few, trifling steps ahead,*
>   *And nearer to the end,*
> *So that you, too, once past the bend,*
> *Shall meet again, as face to face this friend*
>   *You fancy dead.*

> *Push gayly on, strong heart: The while*
> *You travel forward mile by mile,*
> *He loiters with a backward smile*
>   *Till you can overtake,*
> *And strains his eyes, to search his wake*
> *Or, whistling, as he sees you through the brake*
>   *Waits on a stile.*

Her hair was white; her cheeks, though pink, were covered with a network of deep, crisscrossed lines. The little girl who had come to see her pondered all this and then asked gravely, "Are you an old lady?"

"No, honey," her eyes, bright with an unconquerable spirit, held a twinkle. "Not exactly. But I must say I've been young for a mighty long time."

It is indeed hard to have to grow old, perhaps we should say older, even harder than to grow up. There is no way of stopping the inevitable slowing down of bodily processes, the loss of physical flexibility. But, happily for all of us, while we lose the outward signs of youth, it is yet possible to retain forever that same buoyant, hopeful spirit that filled our earlier years. Fortunately our most rewarding capacities, for companionship, for love, for creativeness, for intellectual activity, for a thousand other of the plain, simple enjoyments of life, need not be diminished one whit with the passage of years.

But there is no guarantee that this will be so. It is a goal that has to be worked for actively and with courage and great determination and, most of all, with faith in our ability to master the difficulties that passing time puts in our way. As we age we must, more than ever before, weigh our own personalities with utter frankness, and have a sincere desire to change those qualities which, having weighed, we find wanting. If we do not, we are in trouble. The bad traits we had in our youth often become even more accentuated with the years, and the inner conflicts which we have left unsolved an increasingly heavy burden to us.

There is a time in our lives when sheer drive and energy, or beauty in the case of women, overshadows such traits as selfishness, or irritability, or an insistence on dominating others. But when that youthful drive, or that loveliness of youth, is gone, unpleasant traits have a way of standing out with startling clarity. In the middle years and beyond, deficiencies of personality not only become increasingly and painfully obvious but also have a tendency to assert themselves more and more, until they take over the whole personality.

The person inclined, at twenty-six, to repeat his jokes occasionally or tell over-long stories, may become an interminable bore at sixty. The short-tempered, irritable youngster who is merely an annoyance to his friends becomes, if he is not careful, a hopelessly angry and irascible old man, shunned by all. An exaggerated but rather harmless sense of economy in youth may develop into a contemptible miserliness. Or an overinclination to worry may develop in the final years into a shattering state of anxiety.

We recall, for example, a man who at thirty had been constantly afraid that he would not have enough money to support himself and his family. Although he was more successful than most men of his age, that had had little effect on his anxiety. To a certain extent his particular form of worrying could be traced to the fact that he had been brought up in poverty, by erratic parents, but his real trouble lay not in the poverty, but in the profound emotional insecurity which they had rooted in his unconscious mind and which colored every aspect of his life. Paradoxically, the more money he made, the greater his anxiety became.

By the time he was seventy he had accumulated close to half a million dollars which, put into gilt-edged investments, brought him more than enough income to take care of any imaginable need. Despite this, nothing could shake his apprehension that he was going to end his days as a pauper. He would call his broker almost daily to inquire anxiously about the state of the market and to suggest some new changes in his holdings. What had in his youth passed for a slightly excessive interest in money became in his old age an obsession that completely destroyed his peace of mind. He became a querulous, pathetic person whom everyone avoided.

Before we reach even the middle years, it is wise to

stop and take stock of ourselves. There is still time enough to alter those tendencies in the character which we have managed to gloss over in the past but which will, if not remedied now, cause real unhappiness later. And there is still time to cultivate those character traits which will help us to grow older happily. Our happiness and well-being depend on those attitudes which will gain for us the love and respect of our families and friends. We need to cultivate generosity, kindness, unselfishness, sympathy, tolerance, an appreciation of the value of every individual as an individual, and a willingness to let other people think and feel differently than we do without becoming angry at them. And, above all, we need to cultivate the ability to listen. These are qualities of mind and heart which will enrich the passing years. Such attitudes, if they are deeply ingrained in our personalities, will not diminish as our physical powers inevitably must. But, without them, we invited a sad, embittered loneliness.

Virtues also, fortunately, multiply themselves as the years advance. An old man, in his nineties, had become quite feeble. As sometimes happens in advanced age, a degeneration of the brain cells had dimmed his memory to the extent that he no longer even recognized his few remaining old friends.

In his youth he had been unusually courteous and kindly, the sort of person who never failed in gracious courtesy. It was interesting to see how this basic character structure of his remained unaltered, even in his rather pitiable physical state. Shortly before his death, a friend went to visit him and was shown into his room by a nurse. The old man got to his feet at once and said politely, "Won't you have this chair, please? How are you, sir?"

"Don't you remember me? I'm John," his visitor said.

There was not even the faintest look of recognition on the old man's face. But he smiled and said, "Yes, yes. Of course. I'm so glad to see you." Then he picked up a box of candy from the table and extended it to his friend, inquiring after his health. He did not recognize him, but his impulse was as always to put him at ease, to make him feel at home, and to offer him whatever he had. Even though his mind had deteriorated physically, he still retained those outgoing traits which had been characteristic of him during his whole earlier life.

The displacing of unpleasant and destructive attitudes with pleasant and creative ones is a most urgent task of the middle years. Another, and no less important task, is the combatting of a certain cynicism which frequently assails one at this time. The most dangerous pitfall in the process of growing older is this disillusionment and lack of faith. Perhaps youthful hopes and ideals have not been fulfilled completely. But while there once seemed to be still endless time and opportunity to accomplish one's dream, to wipe out every failure, the realization now comes, inevitably, that this is no longer so. And the tendency is to retreat into disillusionment, and into cynicism, as if one were saying, "It is not I who failed life, but life that failed me."

It may well be that now it is essential to re-examine all of these goals once set for ourselves. We dreamed of achieving certain results which we measured in terms of wealth, possessions, power, prestige, love, or of leadership in business or community affairs. In the flush of adolescence, or in early adulthood, it all looked so very foolproof! How could we miss? But now, not having fully gained these heights, what looks to us like undue failure imparts a sharp bitterness to the cup of passing years.

And yet, very often, if we view our achievements with true perspective and are really fair and reasonable, we find that we have often accomplished other and equally satisfying things to replace those which we once desired but have not accomplished. The only sensible course now, in the middle years, is to re-evaluate and to modify the goals, and bring them in line with what experience has shown us we can reasonably expect to accomplish. They may not be as high as they once were; they will have the virtue of being realistic. It may be, even, that we will find we no longer even aspire to them. Perhaps the new goals may be of finer quality and will therefore lead to greater satisfaction.

Some of the more apparent physical changes which come in the forties are a hard blow to many people, harder to take, often, than lack of unqualified success, particularly to those who have taken great pride in their physical charm, or in their sheer energy or strength. Baldness, graying hair, wrinkles that spread their net from eyes to forehead and finally to the whole face, flabbiness of figure, all viewed with daily despair in the mirror, are taken as proof that the best of life is finished. Our contemporary civilization places a false emphasis on the value of youth and beauty as compared to other virtues. Advertisements, the motion pictures and much popular fiction din into our minds the superficial idea that surface loveliness is what really counts.

Men, sensing a loss of strength and virility, fruitlessly and pathetically assert that they are "as good as they ever were." But in the physical sense, and of course only that, they are not. They may play thirty-six holes of golf, or six sets of tennis in the broiling sun to prove the unprovable. But they are just letting their feeling of inferiority drive them to excesses which, unhappily, often result in physical injury.

The same fear of losing their grip may drive them to overcompensate in other directions. It is not uncommon, for example, to see men in their forties get involved in a series of flirtations with women much younger than themselves. It is frequently observed that men who have led straightforward, sane lives sometimes suddenly embark on extramarital affairs that violate their consciences and the moral standards they have faultlessly adhered to until now.

In their self-induced blindness they are unable to see the one all-important truth which can guide them through the difficult, complicated period of growing older: that real, lasting charm and beauty and virility exist not primarily in the body but in the spirit. The most effective prescription for growing older with success and dignity is a steady, persistent development of one's inner resources.

A charming old lady, a gay and radiant person, was a member of the Marble Collegiate Church. She was a native New Yorker, born and brought up in a brownstone house a few blocks north of Washington Square. When she was young, a girl was hired by her family as a maid.

The two young women became devoted and inseparable companions and continued so during the rest of their lives. It was a friendship that their differing economic statuses did not affect.

One day when a friend came to call, the old lady said, "I had a most curious experience this morning. I saw myself in a mirror in a way that I never really had before. I was quite startled! I looked at that old, old person in the mirror and I said to myself, 'Surely that's not I! Surely I don't look like that! I certainly don't feel like that!' I was astonished! I realized at last that I am old—an old woman, like my mother before me, but that I simply hadn't felt a bit different from the way I always had."

Her maid, and lifelong friend, commented as the visitor was leaving. "I looked at her today as she said that. And she really has not changed; she is just the same as she was on that spring morning fifty years ago." Seen through the eyes of genuine affection, there is no change; the body grows old, but the spirit need not. The real person need never deteriorate under the decaying effects of time.

Most people who age before their time do so not because of stiffening joints or muscles, but because of stiffening minds which become rigid with intolerance, and irritability, and selfishness. But as long as the mind remains alert, flexible, tolerant, and undominated by hatred and resentment, it can function at peak efficiency well beyond three score years and ten.

The athlete is soon "old," because his standards are those set for muscles. But the brain worker, the musician, the chemist, the engineer, for example, need never be. A baseball star's prowess fades in his late thirties; but a writer, such as Somerset Maugham, may be powerfully productive in his seventies. The fine coordination of eye, muscle and nerve may lose its sharp edge, but the creative mind and soul gather experience and skill from year to year. They become stronger and more resourceful. But, for this to happen, the person must become wiser and more honest with himself.

And so the wise person, as he grows older, must turn to the perfecting of his creative and appreciative abilities, which mellow and improve with age. He must take inventory of his personality, realizing that whatever it is now, so it will tend to be in later years, multiplied many times.

Ask yourself these nine determinative questions:

1. Am I self-centered, or do I take other people's needs and desires into account as well as my own?

2. Am I intolerant of other people, and other opinions that differ from mine, or am I prepared to concede that others, as well as myself, have a right to their own habits and beliefs; in short, can I live and let live?

3. Am I constantly irritated by large or small annoyances, or do I take things as they come with a minimum of friction?

4. Do I maintain an unrelenting, high-speed, high-pressure pace, or have I learned the inestimable value of setting aside some time each day for complete mental and physical relaxation?

5. Do I have real resources within myself or am I forever trying to escape my own thoughts and feelings, depending on others to entertain and amuse me?

6. Am I growing a crop of hatreds and resentments to sour and embitter my life or do love and affection dominate my relationships with others?

7. Does an appeal for help make me close my mind and pocketbook, or am I generous with my time and money when the cause is good?

8. Do worry and guilt gnaw at my peace of mind, or am I content to do my best to solve each problem as it comes, forgetting past failures, and, in the spirit of St. Paul, to say calmly, ". . . and having done all . . . stand."

9. Lastly, do I merely pay lip service to the principles of my religion, or are they a practical, dynamic part of my daily, even hourly, life?

It is easy to be overalarmed about one's health; and so it is wise to take a physical inventory and, thereafter, to have a complete medical checkup at regular intervals. It is all too easy to lay physical ills to mental habits and, conversely, to lay mental and emotional ills to physical conditions. But it is a wise person who knows his own physical resources as well as his limitations. Daily habits should be suited to the body requirement in all such things as food and rest and exercise. The body needs normal, sensible care; it is no more to be rejected than the rest of the earth that we live in. But if a person would look the part of a healthy, attractive human being, regardless of age, the important thing is the conquering of worry, and resentment, and bitterness, all of which show in the face and in the attitude.

There is an old puritanical feeling that as one approaches the end of life he should grow long-faced and morose. That is a crime against our Lord, in whom St. Paul told us to "Rejoice . . . and again I say, rejoice." If the person at middle age has not learned the art of happiness he should start at once to practice enjoying life. It is a duty he owes the rest of the world as well as himself.

Very often people tell us that each year when spring comes around again, and the air is soft, when the ground grows warm under the sun, and the trees begin to leaf, they say to themselves, "I'm getting old now. There won't be many more springtimes for me like this, not many more days when I will have that wonderful feeling that spring has come again!" And they are sad and lonely. What a foolish way to greet the spring!

True, no one can be sure, ever, that he will see even one more spring; but brooding on the transitory nature of his existence on earth will not help. Leave that to God, for your years are in His hands. Take the years He gives and be thankful for them. It is a good philosophy to extract from every fleeting moment the joy and pleasure that it offers. At any period in our lives, and above all in our later years, we certainly should take as our motto: *Live one day at a time*. We should learn to utilize each day to the full, being glad for what it does bring. Each day is a gem to be enjoyed for its own value. Look neither backward nor forward, but savor the full loveliness of the present.

If the present day be filled with pain and trouble, look for the value it offers, and remember He said, "I am with you always." A sure recipe for despair and bitterness in old age is to mar the happiness of the present by apprehension and gloom about how many days are left in the future. This can lead only to cynicism, or to a hard sophistication, or to an injurious anxiety.

We need to retain a childlike wonder before the mysteries and beauties of life, which are indeed everlasting and beyond our understanding: the ancient but ever new miracles of sunrise and sunset, of birth and death, and of young flowers budding in the green spring.

Interests and hobbies which do not require arduous physical exertion will stand us in good stead as our physical energies grow less. One's bent may be for photography, music, sketching, gardening, cabinetmaking, fishing, or the spectator sports like football or baseball. God made this wonderful world and put us here to enjoy it. Aging cannot take from us our right to savor its thrills and beauties. And people who know how to enjoy life can never be cheated by age. We should learn in our youth to participate in the whole good feast God has prepared for us, not just to nibble at its edges. If we really are a part of the world we live in, we can enjoy it, no matter how many or how few the years that are left.

Young or old, our greatest interest tends always to center in ourselves. But now is the time to give that up; it is a luxury that the aging cannot afford! By building up interests completely outside of ourselves, aches and pains and unhappiness can be minimized. Self-centeredness is a deadly disease that destroys the creative outgoing part of us. The more points at which we touch the world around us, the more tendrils of affection we send out from our hearts, the less likely we are to wither in spirit.

In our clinic work we constantly see self-absorbed, cynical, and cantankerous people become transformed by finding an interest, a goal, to which they can devote themselves with disinterested enthusiasm.

A man of about fifty, who looked much older, complained of feeling very nervous and unable to sleep. A medical examination had shown there was nothing organically wrong with him. Thoroughly discontented with his life and with himself, he felt that his time had just about run out. Certainly there seemed nothing left that gave him any real pleasure.

He had been married, though he had no children, and a good many years previously his wife had gone away with another man. He had been left with a savage bitterness

toward the world and everyone in it. For the past ten
years he had lived by himself and for himself. In his opinion there was no one who could be trusted. He simply endured life. He hated it and was waiting to die.

Practically his only social contacts were through his
yearly attendance at his college reunions, for his college
was one of the few things about which he was not utterly
disillusioned. After several talks with him, we suggested
that he might want to do something for his college: setting up a scholarship, for instance, for some boy who
could not afford tuition. This appealed to him and he did
it.

He began to take a personal interest in the first youngster he helped in this way. And, since he had a generous
income, he could afford to expand his new-found activity.
Before too long a time he was making it financially possible for no less than twelve boys to go through college.
This became the paramount interest in his life. He
thought of these boys as his sons, and he loved them as
much as if they had been his own. In ten years he not
only helped send nearly a hundred boys through college,
but also gave many of them a start in business or professional life.

The change in him was truly remarkable. His nervousness and tenseness disappeared. He began to sleep well.
And he now weighed what he should weigh. Most important of all, he was really happy. Getting an interest outside of himself had brought about a rejuvenation of his
body and mind. This process literally transformed his life.
He forgot himself, but scores of men will never forget
him!

In the clinic we encounter a great many single men and
women in their forties and fifties who, not having married,
see their hopes for a home and family receding to the
vanishing point. They live, most of them, in Y.M. or
Y.W.C.A.'s, in residence clubs and various other kinds of
bachelor quarters. And, their lives being turned inward,
they are apt to become lonely and bitter.

Many of them come to us filled with anxiety and depression, sadly convinced that the future promises them
nothing. With too much time by themselves spent in

gloomy retrospection and endless, fruitless hashing over of their personal problems, they fall victim to a host of psychological disorders. Their great need, of which they are usually very conscious, is to build friendships that will give them an outlet for their love and affection.

To help them, we have set up in connection with the church what we call "forty-plus" and "fifty-plus" clubs. Here they find the congenial companionship of people of the same age and often with much the same interests. More often than not that is all that they need to recover from their feeling of futility. But this therapy of fellowship they do need most desperately. Man, after all, is not meant to be alone; he is fundamentally a group-living animal. To violate this law of his nature can only bring distress.

But, if the first crucial point in growing older comes in the late forties, when various physical changes become marked, a second equally critical point is reached in the middle and late sixties, when one must prepare himself spiritually and psychologically for the final pull.

According to the statistical tables, a man or woman who has survived to the age of sixty no longer has a life expectancy of the Biblical three score and ten years, but one of four score or more—he or she may live to eighty or over. Therefore, the years after sixty may very well be a full fourth of the person's life. The first quarter of our lives was, or so it seemed to us, spent in getting ready to live. It would be a stupid affront to the Creator if the last quarter were to be spent in getting ready to die!

Of course many people must retire from their life work at sixty-five, even though they feel at the height of their power, and they look on this as a savage tragedy. Certainly one of the hardest situations faced at this time is that of retirement. Eventually society will be shocked at the waste of trained resource thus imposed on itself. But at present there is not much to do but accept it and adjust to it.

Those of us who know that retirement from our job at a specific age is necessary should face that fact well ahead of time and plan for it, rather than evade it until the very last moment. And instead of feeling angry and perturbed and jealous of those who will take the place left vacant, we should try to accept it philosophically and put our energies into planning some fruitful and interesting program, not just a "hobby," which will enrich our last years. This time of life should be planned in advance. It has been our observation that people who retire and do nothing just about sign their own death warrant, if not of the body, then at least of the spirit.

A man of sixty-five had been retired from a top executive job in a large firm. He was dazed and depressed; he was lost and forlorn.

"I've been an exceptionally busy man all my life," he told us. "It's always been my great delight to make decisions, to plan new enterprises, and to see them work out. Well, I haven't done a single thing of importance for a whole year! When I see my friends who are still active in business, they seem to belong to a different world. They're polite, but they haven't much time for me. When I go to my club, I'm bored. My wife is dead, and my children are grown up and lead their own lives, in which I don't want to intrude. What is there left for me?

"You ask me what I think I would like to do? I don't know. That's the trouble! I just don't know."

But after several conferences, he said one day, "I've been thinking. There's a little bank in my home town, and I've heard they're having a pretty tough time getting by. Perhaps I should buy some stock in that bank and become one of its officers."

He investigated the matter and shortly afterward did become an officer of this bank. For the eight remaining years of his life he led a happy, useful, and successful existence. People in that town went to him when they were in trouble. Often, when they lacked the qualifications for credit from the bank, he loaned them money out of his own pocket. And he helped several young men to set themselves up in business. He became such a powerful and greatly loved force for good that when he died he was mourned by the whole community. He once said, "When I retired I thought I had finished my life's work. But now I know this was also part of the whole."

Another man who had let retirement creep up on him without preparation came to us in a similar state of agitation, feeling that his life was unendurable.

We talked over all his many interests and found that, among other things, he had always been an avid sportsman. But now killing birds and animals had become distasteful to him; so we suggested that he make use of his skill and knowledge about wild life in a somewhat different way.

He took up the scientific study of bird life at a museum of natural history. Before long he was organizing field expeditions and directing campaigns of public education on the protection of migratory birds. For many years his life was fascinating and filled with adventure. But more than than, he made a real contribution to the conservation of the country's game bird resources, and to the lives of the other people that he interested in it.

There is another large group of people who have retirement forced upon them without realizing that they should be so classed. They are the women whose lives have been entirely occupied with the managing of their homes and who at the death of their husbands find themselves with incomes of one value or another but without responsibility, as formerly. This is a very hard form of "retirement" to face in advance, of course, because it involves thinking about the death of another person. But women should not only ask themselves the question, "What would I do if I had to make a living?" but also "What would I do with my life if I were forced by circumstances to lead it without my partner?" Knitting does not prove to be enough! Clubs do not prove to be enough! Even social service and charity may not be enough! And, like the retired man who finds that his old friends have little time for him, she may also find that she falls into the category of outsider.

Every woman should sit down just as every man should and make a list of all the interesting forms of possible occupation. And after careful study she should select one and prepare for it as if her life depended on it, as indeed, her spiritual life may.

There is no reason why a man and his wife might not sit down and work out a retirement program together.

Not just the matter of funds, which they often do, but the occupation also. Many have followed this advice and testify to the wisdom of it.

A garage mechanic and his wife retired and ran a gas station in a midwestern state. They closed their station at six o'clock and went off to night school together, he carrying her books. They were taking a course in accounting and in finance.

Another couple slipped away from an important office in the bank each afternoon in their limousine and had the chauffeur put them down at a school for restaurant management. The day after his retirement they planned to open a gourmet's paradise.

But however it may be done, everyone should evolve some suitable program of action that will profitably occupy his time and give value and meaning to the final years. This can be made the richest experience in life, "the last for which the first was made."

But no matter how vigorously one attacks life, no matter how consistently one refuses to be whipped by it, there comes inevitably the time when life has a tendency to run down and grow stale. As long as one wakes up each morning and eagerly thinks what great things may happen that very day, one is young. But when the first waking thought is, "Well, it's just the same old grind. One more round of the same old things. Nothing good or different can happen to me today, nothing but more of the same," then something has gone out of life. When that attitude gets to be a chronic state, age has really overtaken a person, no matter what the sum of the years may be. The creative process has unwound itself; the spring has gone out of life. It has run down.

So the ideas need to be freshened up. There is a desperate need for a new sense of adventure and eagerness. It takes a true re-creation to restore the old zest and the old pleasure in living. The cause of this feeling of dullness may be family burdens, business cares, routine, monotony, or just plain disillusionment: but these are all of the spirit, and they indicate that the spirit is in trouble.

The cure is to drink again of the Eternal Fountain of

energy and interest which is God. One must bring God into the very center of his life. When this is done, the vitality and the sense of wonder and boundless enthusiasm will be restored. Both the mind and the heart will be renewed.

There is a professor in a small university who has been there for so long that he is now an institution like its vine-covered buildings.

"I want to tell you something I've learned through the years," he once said to his class. "I am an old man. I've watched you youngsters come here and graduate and go away. And then much later I've watched you return. Some of you girls were pretty when you left, but you came back after not many years looking haggard and hard. Some of you were not very pretty in your school years, but you came back really beautiful.

"Some of the pretty girls will still be pretty when they come back, and some of the homely ones will still be homely. But I'll tell you something: The ones who are really pretty years later will be the ones who have learned to know God. There will be a light in their faces, and a loveliness in their eyes, and a softness and sweetness about them that doesn't come any other way. As the saying goes, 'Beauty shines out of the countenance when love is in the heart.' And the finest cosmetic in the world flows from a consecrated and contented spirit."

A woman of fifty-five had been a semi-invalid for nearly ten years. She was unable to sleep at all well, and had lost so much weight that she was distressing to see. She was a most bitter, and cynical, and hostile woman. In the college in which she worked, her assistants were terrified of speaking to her for fear of being flayed by the sharp, slashing phrases she so delighted in directing at them.

It is strange the way great events may suddenly take place in our lives. One Sunday she went to church. It was the first time in many years. It so happened that the sermon struck a live spark in her. It seemed to stir something in the very depths of her mind. She was shaken by it. It set in motion a real spiritual reawakening. She had the feeling, as she expressed it, that a barrier had all at once been burned away inside of her. And as a result she became profoundly changed.

Time deepened and solidified the force of this powerful religious experience. Instead of an ugly tension, there was a really beautiful radiance in her face. In three months she had regained twenty pounds and was sleeping perfectly. She was still witty, and she was still sharp-tongued when she needed to be, but the old unhealthy meanness and bitterness was gone.

At a dinner party one evening, the most energetic and engaging person present was a man of ninety with snow-white hair. He fairly bubbled with gaiety and good humor. He laughed and talked, and made others laugh and talk. When someone tried to bring up a gloomy subject, he diplomatically sidetracked it.

"War? Hard times? Let's worry about them if and when they happen!"

The person sitting next to him, amazed at this man's vitality, said to him, "You really have the gift of living! Are you always as happy as this?"

"Yes. Surely," the old man said. "But I'll tell you, I was not always so. For many years I was a very unhappy man! I was sick with wretchedness!

"But fifty years ago I got well! I was cured! Do you know how? I found a text in the Bible. It was a great text, a magnificent text! And I took it to live by, and it made my life over. 'They that wait upon the Lord shall renew their strength; they shall mount up with wings as eagles; they shall run, and not be weary; and they shall walk, and not faint.' "

"Do you actually think a text, a few words, could do that for you?" he was asked.

"Think it? I don't think it, I know it. Those words sank down into my gloomy and diseased thoughts and healed my mind. When I began to think differently I became a different person. I learned to get joy out of life and even at ninety I get wonderful happiness out of living."

To meet life as successfully in old age as in youth, we must rid ourselves of those vestiges of immaturity which may even then, at the end of life, be a barrier to adjustment and to faith. We must root out of the personality those neurotic traits which distort our view of the world around us and magnify its terrors and make us cringe before its blows. One who is crippled by a sense of guilt, by wide fluctuations between love and hate, by anxiety, tension, and depression, by a blind fear of death, or worst of all by a lack of faith, can never fulfill his destiny in his youth, his middle age, or his final years.

Psychiatry and religion, joined together, point a way to the solution of these pressing difficulties. One who will fortify himself with insight into the feelings and thoughts which lie in the unconscious mind can with a clear affirmative faith in God face with confidence every period and every problem of life.

To live with power and to achieve self-fulfillment is to bring God from the shadowy edges of the mind into its bright center. It is to master the most demanding and yet the most rewarding of all human achievements, the art of real happiness.

XI *How to make the most of you*

"Am I doing what I really ought to be doing?" "Am I being my real self?" These are the queries of many of us who wonder if we are making the best of our opportunities, or are unhappy about our living conditions, or just generally confused about the complexities of modern life. We all have unfulfilled dreams and yearnings. Each of us feels at times that life has passed us by, and we don't know how to catch up with it.

Twenty years ago a young Negro came to New York City from the South. He was filled with ambition. "My dream was to make a lot of money, own a flashy car, wear expensive clothes and have a pocketful of fifty-cent cigars," he recalled to friends recently.

But the only job he could find was that of a Red Cap in Grand Central Station. He did not want it. He felt that carrying bags for other people was beneath him. He wanted to give orders, not take them. Only because of financial necessity did he finally take the position. Then, for several years he worked as a Red Cap, seething at the way some people spoke to him, snarling to himself about the smallness of tips, snapping at his fellow workers when they displeased him.

Unhappy, feeling that he was missing something, this Red Cap reluctantly turned, as many do in such a situation, to the church. "I went to find out if God could help me achieve all the things I wanted in life," he admits candidly. "When I prayed, I asked for a better job, success, more money."

His prayers for material things were not answered. This Red Cap might have continued his restless search elsewhere if he had not lingered long enough in church to make contact with the greatest source of power the Christian church has to offer. For the ultimate answers to life's dissatisfactions are not found in the church building itself, nor through church people regardless of how good they may be, nor even in the words and advice of the minister. Jesus Christ is the heart and soul of the Christian church; in Him and through Him do Christians find the real answer to loneliness, frustration, and unhappiness.

The Red Cap was attracted to the Master of Life, and the challenge in these words, "If any man be in Christ, he is a new creature: old things are passed away; behold all things are become new." (II Corinthians 5:17)

The all-important change in the Red Cap's life came when he realized that it was not what Christ could do *for* him that really mattered, but what Christ could do *through* him. For Christ must work *through* people if He is to transform lives. The Red Cap didn't come to this conclusion without much prayer and reading of the Scriptures. The result of months of spiritual searching was this prayer:

"Lord, I asked You before for a better job and more money, I see now that You *did* answer my prayer. The answer was 'No.' Since then I have learned my limitations, but I am not frustrated by this knowledge. I have had the wonderful experience of bringing Christ into my life. 'Old things are passed away.' I no longer want a new job if You think I can serve You best as a Red Cap. Please show me how to use my work for the glory of Your Kingdom."

From that moment Ralston Young, Red Cap 42, started to make the most of his job. His mental attitude changed from "How much of a tip will I get" to "How can I help carry this man's troubles as well as his bags?"

As a result, he started noonday prayer services in a railroad coach on Track 13 in Grand Central Station. The simple, informal inspiration of these meetings soon drew people from all stations in life, regardless of position, color, or faith.

Slowly the lay ministry of this humble Red Cap grew. He was asked to talk to small church groups; more recently he has accepted speaking invitations to such colleges as Yale and Vassar, even though he never had a college education. Always his message is simple yet eloquent testimony of how Christ works through people.

Ralston Young is a remarkable example of a man equipped with average abilities who is making the maximum use of his life. He did it by using a formula for living that is available to all of us. You might call it the "technique of making the most of you." To develop this technique, first take a realistic survey of your God-given talents. Then dedicate these talents to God, praying that He will use them in the best way possible. Meanwhile go about life normally, alert to every opportunity for service.

Taking a realistic survey of one's God-given talents is more difficult than it appears. People think that they know themselves, but they really do not. They are usually ignorant of the complexity of their intellectual and emotional lives.

This was true of a twenty-five-year-old girl whom we will call Janet. She was a most pathetic figure when she seated herself inside our counseling room at the clinic. Janet was rather large; she had short chubby fingers which were clenched around a sodden handkerchief. There were dark circles under her eyes and while talking she had trouble controlling her voice.

"I came to your clinic," she told us, "because I am afraid I will kill myself unless someone helps me."

Then, between sobs, Janet told us a story we hear often in one form or another. She had come to New York to make a career for herself as a concert pianist. In a Greenwich Village apartment, she had found a teacher who had worked with her for nearly four years. "She kept encouraging me," Janet said. "Even when I wondered about my ability, she told me that I could become a great pianist if only I would work harder. But every time I asked her if I were ready for an audition, she kept putting me off. Several weeks ago I met a man who is a piano accompanist. I told him of my ambition and asked if I could play for him."

Janet paused again, to control her voice. "I played for him. I thought I did very well. He was nice about it, but he said I was wasting my time, because I just didn't have the ability to be a concert pianist.

"I was furious with him, of course," she continued. "So I went to see another music teacher. She agreed with the accompanist. Then I had it out with my own teacher, who blew up at me, called me names and said she would have nothing more to do with me.

"Now I don't know what to do or where to turn. I can't go home and face my parents and friends. I've told my parents a lot of lies, you see. They think I have already made public appearances. I had to make them think I was getting ahead so they would keep sending me money for lessons and living expenses. Now I feel I would be better off dead."

Janet's problem was more pathetic than tragic. Yet others in such circumstances have committed suicide rather than admit failure and deception to family and friends.

The most surprising angle in Janet's case was how she became interested in the piano at all. Questioning brought out these facts: as a child she had taken piano lessons only because her mother had requested her to. Her piano teacher then had given her no encouragement. She had never particularly liked music. At school she remembered once getting a D in music; one teacher had told her she was a little tone deaf.

This case is significant because it shows how some people waste many years of their lives trying to achieve something they are not equipped to do. Janet had no real talent for music. Her mother, frustrated because she herself couldn't have a music career, had wrongly propelled her daughter into this field.

The psychiatrist in this case helped Janet make a difficult reappraisal of her real talents through self-analysis. Most people have the mistaken notion that self-analysis is self-criticism. Ask the average person to analyze himself and he will name all his defects. But self-analysis, properly understood, involves self-appreciation as well as self-criticism. It should point up our good qualities as well as our weaknesses.

"God has made each of us a distinct separate individual with ability to do certain things in a way no one else can," the minister explained at a subsequent session. "Don't selfishly cheat both yourself and your fellow men of the true God-intended you," he told her. "Find the field where your talents can come into bloom."

Janet, it came out, did have another special interest. Children. A part-time job was found for her in the children's ward of a hospital. The last we heard of Janet, she had married and now has children of her own. Janet had great difficulty taking a realistic view of her own talents, but once she did, she became an entirely new person.

Once this first step of self-evaluation is completed, the next can begin. Dedicate your talents to God and pray that God will use them in the best way possible. Every person born on this earth can, through faith, prayer, and guidance, find a useful, even important, niche to fill.

Helen Keller was struck with brain fever at the age of two. At first doctors held little hope that she would live, but she did recover. But from that time on she was both deaf and blind. Who would have thought this child could ever amount to anything? What Helen Keller accomplished with a bare minimum of personal assets is one of the greatest stories of our age. When she celebrated her 77th birthday recently, Miss Keller was tirelessly serving the blind and blind-deaf, traveling over the world, writing and lecturing. She had written a dozen books which have been translated into 50 languages. She is the direct inspiration for 50 schools for the blind, 44 state-supported schools, and 48 state programs for the blind.

"I have struggled like everybody else to find myself and enter a field of usefulness," Miss Keller wrote recently in *Guideposts Magazine*. "I believe that we begin heaven now and here if we do our work for others faithfully. There is no useful work that is not part of the welfare of mankind. Even the humblest occupation is skilled labor if it contains an effort above mere self-support to serve a spiritual or social need."

You can get out of life only what you are. As Ernest Holmes stated, "The getting is in the being, and the being always begets the getting; child will be like parent, and men do not gather grapes from cacti. If we want to use the power in our minds, we have to realize it is a spiritual power. We have to realize we are living in a spiritual universe. This means that right now, at the center of everything God is enthroned. And it was Browning who said that our task is to 'loose this imprisoned splendor.' "

In other words, God created man in His Image to achieve great things. But "great things" for the grammar school arithmetic teacher, who inspires children with an excitement to learn, would not be "great things" for the scientific genius Einstein, who delved deeply into the basic mysteries of the universe. Man must accept his limitations and still not dull his incentive to use what abilities he has in a maximum way.

In *Faith Is the Answer* we told the story of Ike Skelton, Jr., who at 13 was stricken with the most virulent form of polio. But the lad had a strong faith and a stout heart. He pulled through, but with complete paralysis of both arms. This calamity seemed to end forever Ike's dream of athletic accomplishments.

Ike refused to accept such a verdict. Since running was one of the few sports he could compete in for his school, Wentworth Academy, without use of arms, he decided to become a two-miler. For months he trained conscientiously. In the big race against his school's arch rival, Ike was entered in the two-mile run. He ran his heart out. When he staggered across the finish line, teammates and spectators swept him up on their shoulders, and he got the biggest ovation of the day—*in spite of the fact that he had finished last.*

A woman who read this account of Ike's recovery wrote a somewhat critical letter to the authors, saying that she had a husband attempting a long and painful recovery from a severe case of polio. "I don't want my husband to read the story about Ike Skelton, Jr.," she said. "It would discourage him to hear that a boy of Ike's courage and patience worked so hard on his running only to be last in the race."

The woman, of course, missed the whole point of the story. Ike won a greater victory that day than any other boy competing in the track meet. He was the only boy on the field with a hundred percent performance—whose ability met his capacity. Everyone recognized it—that's why there was a tremendous ovation for him. Yet, it was soon obvious, of course, that Ike's primary role in life was not to become a runner. And the polio-stricken boy soon accepted that fact.

Recently, we heard more about Ike Skelton, Jr., from his mother. "After he graduated from Wentworth," she wrote, "several painful operations gave him partial use of his right arm. Two years ago he won an exchange scholarship to the University of Edinburgh (Scotland). He went over alone and came back with honors. Last year he got his A.B. degree from the University of Missouri, where he made Phi Beta Kappa and was the highest ranking boy in Arts and Sciences. He is now at law school and is writing for the Law Review, which only high-ranking students are permitted to do.

"But the most wonderful blessing of all," Mrs. Skelton continued, "is the way Ike has accepted his physical limitations. He is always smiling and happy. He spoke recently at Christian College on the topic 'The Unseen Evidence.' President Miller told me afterward that they had had all kinds of speakers, but none better than Ike."

In their search for happiness some individuals steadfastly refuse to accept themselves. They dislike their own personality so much that they try to copy the mannerisms of others. The result is almost always harmful to persons who do this. It stands to reason that if you try to copy someone else, you will never be as good as that person, because you are admitting at the start that he or she is better than you are. But the one thing you can do better than anyone else is to be yourself.

"The Lord gave you certain qualities which are more attractive in you than anyone else," one woman was told by the minister here at our clinic recently. She felt she needed an entirely new personality to be a success. It was pointed out to her that Will Rogers was always an Oklahoma cowboy. He mastered the art of being himself in every situation that came along. People loved him for this very naturalness. But a keenly efficient and methodical man like Douglas MacArthur would have been ridiculed if he acted like Will Rogers. Jimmy Durante would never have achieved success if he had changed from the East Side boy with the big nose.

Russell Nype, who made such a hit in the play *Call Me Madam a* few years ago, told this interesting story about himself. In his high school and college days, Russell felt he was always on the fringe of the crowd. He longed to be popular, to be in the center, but felt his unattractive appearance and shy personality held him back.

"I paid for expensive contact lenses so that I could see without wearing my hated eye glasses," he admitted. "Then I studiously cultivated the mannerisms of those I thought were the most popular types. I wanted to become an entirely different person."

When Russell Nype went into acting, he spent years copying, in an exaggerated way, the personalities of various male movie stars. But he was rejected for dramatic parts time after time. One day a discerning producer spotted something in young Nype, and he was given a part in *Call Me Madam*.

"Here's the pay-off," Russell revealed. "They had me play a part that was identical to my pre-Broadway self. I had to be shy and wear glasses. I laugh now when I think of it. After all my efforts to be different, here I was finally making good by playing my true self."

The critics hailed Russell Nype for his charm and spontaneity in this role. Today, he is wearing glasses again—and being himself.

If you have certain inferiority feelings and have been trying to become someone you are not, why not play this little game with yourself. Set aside one day a week as a "Be Myself Day." Don't try to impress a single person all day long. Don't attempt anything over your head. Take an honest look at your living standards, friends, and activities. Where are you straining yourself? To make the most of yourself, you must learn the difference between honest hard work and neurotic straining for some false goal. The person who has mastered this difference can be relaxed while hard at work; the person who has not mastered it can be full of stress and strain while on an expenses-paid vacation to Bermuda.

A young man named William Morrisette had a very well-paying position as salesman some years ago, but he wasn't content with himself. He worked hard—that is to say, he put in long hours—and was under constant tension. But deep down inside, Morrisette knew he was going in the wrong direction.

"My heart wasn't in the product I was selling," he admitted. "I loved airplanes. At every spare opportunity, I would drop down to the nearest airport and watch the flying activity. My prime reading interests were aviation. I believe I had always wanted to be with an airline."

One day Morrisette applied for a job at Eastern Air Lines. "They informed me only a few low-paying positions were available," he said. "I told them I liked the spirit of their organization, that I wanted to work for them and didn't care where I started. So they gave me a job." Friends thought Morrisette was out of his mind when he quit as a salesman to work at a much reduced salary in the Eastern Air Lines ticket office.

But for the first time in many years Morrisette was happy with his work. All his ability and energy was now channeled lovingly in one direction. The inevitable result was that he soon climbed in the organization to the point where today he is an Eastern Air Lines Vice-President.

Morrisette discovered the error in straining for a goal that did not satisfy his innermost yearnings. When he put himself in line with God's purpose for his life, he became a new man.

Another salesman—a shoe salesman this time—happened to hear this chance remark one day: "The world has yet to see what God can do with just one man who would give himself completely to service."

"I'll give God the chance," said the salesman, "to do that with me."

He started by going to his local church and asking for a Sunday school class. "I'm sorry," said the minister. "We just haven't got the room. Every classroom is already full to overflowing."

"That's all right," said the shoe salesman. "I'll find a way." He looked over the church building until he found a room that would do. It was the boiler room. Sunday after Sunday, this shoe salesman held classes in the boiler room of the church until the class overflowed. He then went to a local saloon, closed because of the Sabbath and the only other available space in town, and began holding Sunday school classes there. Again attendance outstripped the room. This was the beginning of one of the world's most outstanding ministries. The name of the shoe salesman, who dedicated his abilities to God, was Dwight L. Moody.

Both William Morrisette and Dwight Moody made the most of themselves by a rather dramatic shift in jobs. But not all of us can do that. Some of us are chained to our present occupations by circumstances that are beyond our control. Health, or economic circumstances or family obligations sometimes make it impossible for us to be as free as Morrisette or Moody in changing our work situation.

One such man was Fred Schwartzwalder—a janitor in Colorado—who loves mountains. Schwartzwalder might have become a great mineralogist. But he never had the opportunity for higher education, and even as an adult his job as a janitor did not leave him with much excess cash to use for developing his God-given interest in rocks and minerals. Some men might have fretted and complained that God was not fair to them. Not Fred. He fulfilled himself in his spare time. Every weekend he took off for the mountains near his home in Colorado. He came back tired but satisfied, often carrying samples of interesting rock formations he had found during his treks.

Then came the war, research in the mysteries of uranium, and the resultant frenzied, nationwide search for the precious ore. Fred Schwartzwalder heard the reports and came to the conclusion that there should be uranium in his mountains. The experts laughed at him. Fred began a search on his own. Week after week he brought home rocks that resembled ore samples he had seen. He and his wife saved pennies for a geiger counter, and the wonderful climax to the story is that Fred did find uranium. It is one of the country's richest veins, and it is right where the experts said it couldn't be. Fred Schwartzwalder fulfilled himself even though he had to do it on his spare time.

It is normal for all of us at times to feel a sense of dissatisfaction with our lives. So, too, is it natural to feel confined by a job, even though it is work we like. When these low moments come, ask yourself, "Am I being my real self? Am I using my God-given talents in a maximum way?"

Don't try to take on a completely different personality. Spiritual rebirth, however, where one replaces doubtful values with Christ-like qualities, is much to be desired. This kind of transformation will do much to bring to the surface hidden creative qualities in an individual. It will not make a good financier out of a mechanic—or vice-versa. But, the miraculous transformations you sometimes see in people are usually the result of the development of latent powers which were in these people all the time.

Be your real self; let your God-given qualities develop naturally and you will make the most out of your life.

XII   *The art of getting along with people*

"Why do most individuals fail in a job situation? Not because of their lack of ability or training or their unwillingness to learn and progress. They fail because they cannot adjust satisfactorily to other people."

These are statements by the head of the personnel department of a large corporation. As a man in charge of hiring and firing for many years, he reports that a department gets behind in orders more often because of friction between two key people than because of inefficiency. Wherever people are together—on the job, in the home, yes, even working in a church—there are inevitable frictions and conflicts. The person who knows how to get along with people, whose feelings are not hurt if someone speaks sharply to him, who knows how to stay pleasant and calm in a crisis is usually a more valuable employee than one with more business ability, but who has a reputation for blowing up.

It is pathetic when you are somebody who has to be handled with care. People have to watch out with you. They say this about you: "Be careful or he will get you into trouble."

But, you may object, "I am what I am. That's the way I was born."

On the contrary there is no study of heredity today by which a person can rationalize his unattractive personality. True, a man born with a small stature will never be successful in professional basketball, which is a game for giants. You cannot change certain physical characteristics.

One's habits and personality however, are not inherited. They are developed. What you are now, you made yourself. But if you don't like the way you are now, you can begin re-making yourself by learning the magic in five words which make up a highly effective formula for getting along with others.

Certainly one of the first rules for getting along with people is to know how to *love* them. By love in this case we do not mean romantic love, but a love that has a concern for another's well being, a genuine interest in him or her as a person. If you are not sure how to start loving people, start by loving God.

"But I can't love God," one man with a personality problem admitted. "Fear Him, yes. But how do I learn to love what I fear?"

"Do you believe in God as a Father, as the Creator of

this earth and everything on it, including yourself?" he was asked.

"Yes. I do."

"Has life on the whole been good to you?"

"Yes, on the whole."

"You are grateful then to God for giving you life."

"That's right."

"When someone has been very good to you, you have a warm feeling for that person. This feeling could be described as love."

"I see what you're getting to," the man said. "I do feel grateful to God and perhaps subconsciously I have loved God, but my fear of Him and what He could do to hurt me has overshadowed this love."

"Then you can see that a change in attitude toward God is necessary before you can learn to love Him. And as soon as you feel a real sense of love for God, you will notice that it is easier to love the people around you—people who you must realize are children of God, made in His Image."

By converting his negative thinking habits, this man soon found he had many more reasons to love God than to fear Him. It stands to reason that anyone who can develop a personal loving relationship with God, can also use the same loving relationship in getting along well with people.

The second of these words is *politeness*. A woman, writing to our clinic for advice recently, listed some people who were doing wrong. "I really told them off and no fooling," she said. "They will treat me better or else."

Then, in almost the same breath, she asked, "I want to have more friends, and more faith, but how do I go about it?"

The woman's tone was demanding and ill-mannered. She could see faults in others, but was blind to her own. No wonder she didn't have friends, or a closeness to God.

Many of us stumble this same way. We think we are righteous, we try to do God's work, yet fail to heed St. Paul's reminder: "Be kindly affectioned to one another with brotherly love."

There is more than love of others implied in this advice. The words "kindly affectioned" refer to politeness, without which our relations to family, friends, and neighbors would quickly deteriorate. A person who practices being polite will soon discover he has more love and respect for others. As he finds more of the good in people, his searchings will inevitably come to the perfect example of a gracious and kind man.

Christ realized that when He appeared before people as a leader, they would judge Him first by the qualities of graciousness He possessed. He spoke gently to the people He helped. His concern for the needs of others resulted in the famous scene where He provided loaves and fishes for the multitude. One of His last acts was to wash the feet of His own Disciples.

By contrast, Harry B. was a hard-driving businessman who became successful because of his aggressive tactics. Then he began to have difficulties. He fired his plant manager. One of his close associates quit. There was labor trouble in the factory. Finally, Harry became aware that something in his personality was causing the trouble and he talked to his pastor about it.

"I pay good wages," he said. "No one can say that I'm not generous to my employees. But they don't like me."

"Why do you say that?"

"The plant manager turned them against me. He was a shifty one, that fellow. He played up to the men and took credit for all the improvements we made in working conditions even though he had nothing to do with them. It got so I couldn't stand the sight of him. I wouldn't have fired him, though, if I hadn't caught him stealing equipment. The men think I fired him because he was popular with them. If they want to think that, it's all right with me."

"If you did what you thought was right, the men will eventually find out and respect you for the way you handled the case."

"One thing does bother me, Pastor. Jesus said 'love your enemies, bless them that curse you.' I'm sorry, but I simply cannot love this fellow. Forgive him, yes. But I can tell you right now that you'll be wasting your time if you try to get me to love him."

"Why did your other associate quit?" the minister countered.

"It wasn't because I fired the plant manager. Tom didn't like him any better than I did. Tom is a kind of sensitive guy, and I think the pressure got him down. Sometimes I was short with him and that didn't help. In fact, I'll have to take a lot of the blame here. I could use more patience."

"How do you get along with your secretary?"

Harry made a slight grimace. "To be honest, I find it hard to keep a good secretary. They won't take criticism. I was brought up to be a plain-spoken man, I guess. I never learned a lot of manners because my mother, who could have taught them to me, died while I was a boy."

Harry and the minister then began talking about the relationship of good manners to living a Christian life. "Politeness is a form of Christian love, Harry," said the minister. "You are known for your honesty and forthrightness, but if you mix more graciousness with these qualities you will find you get along better with people."

Several weeks later Harry invited his minister down to the plant. He reported that things were going much more smoothly and the minister asked him why. "I've been thinking over what you told me the other day. I've been working on this business of politeness, and I just wanted to tell you that it works. Because politeness, after all, is just another word for putting-yourself-in-the-other-person's shoes." And with that he pointed to a motto pasted on his desk, which he said was going to be his guide for the future.

It read: "If you can't love your enemies, at least be polite to your friends."

The third word in this formula is *criticism*. In developing the art of getting along with people, one constantly runs into the problem of criticism—both how to give and receive it. No one likes to be criticized, yet we cannot escape it. If we are really honest with ourselves, we know that we do not want to avoid it. Criticism, properly given, enables us to learn and to grow in understanding.

One young writer expressed himself this way: "Most

writers are sensitive to criticism, and I'm certainly no different. It used to burn me up when, after working long hours, lovingly, over a story, some self-appointed critic or ivory-tower editor would tear it to pieces. At first I would either get mad or discouraged. Gradually, I discovered that good criticism was helping me to success. I sought out constructive criticism.

"Today I still wince when something I have labored over is criticized, but my whole approach to the critic has changed. I am grateful that he would take the time to read my stuff and give an opinion. If it is constructive, I am doubly grateful. If I sense personal vindictiveness in any criticism directed at me, I play a little game with myself. Mentally I take the destructive criticism and throw it in the wastebasket, just as I would if it came to me as an anonymous letter. Then washing myself and my pride out of the picture entirely, I say to myself 'Something must be eating this fellow to make these remarks. Perhaps a fight with his wife. Maybe he is having trouble with his job. He might not be in good health.'

"By now I have forgotten myself completely and am concerned with the person who has made the critical remarks. Generally, I follow up this line of mental thinking with a question about his health. In most cases, it does turn out that something is bothering him and which has caused his unkind criticism of me."

Those who have a problem with hurt feelings might find this technique of great value. It will take some mental discipline, but it is based on the sound principle of forgetting self and concerning oneself with others—a practice which will enable anyone to get along better with those with whom he associates.

The ability to give criticism properly is, in some ways, more difficult than to learn how to take it. When a friend, associate or a loved-one is doing something wrong or poorly, it is so easy to say, "He'll learn from experience." Yet this is of little help. Giving constructive criticism is uncomfortable, often difficult to do, but it is a good test of Christian love. And if done right, it will endear you more solidly to people than superficial compliments!

A well-known television personality told recently how

her career was almost ruined at the start because of well-meaning friends. After her first performance, these friends rushed forward to tell her how wonderful she had been.

"Actually, I was terrible," the actress admitted. "But all their compliments made me think I was perfect."

Fortunately, for her, several more realistic friends took her aside, gently told her the facts and encouraged her to work hard to master an art she didn't know. Today, her real gratitude is for the few who were honest with her—rather than the many who just wanted to be nice.

Yet it is so easy to use criticism in the wrong way. A new husband, concerned over the faults he discovered in his bride, hit upon what he thought would be a good way to offer criticism. He took a sheet of paper and wrote the word "Faults" at the top. Then he drew a line down the middle, putting his wife's name on one side and his own on the other.

Then, with much enthusiasm, he began writing all the things wrong with his wife. Somewhat to his surprise the list went to the bottom of the page. When it came to writing down his own faults, however, the going was much slower. When he finished, he placed the paper where he knew his wife would discover it.

Sure enough, the next day when he returned from work, his wife was awaiting him with a glint in her eye. "Did you write this?" she asked shoving the paper under his chin.

"Why yes, dear. I did it as a personal inventory. It's a good idea to take a good look at yourself every now and then," he told her. Then he expected her to take issue with him over the faults he had written under her name. When she did this, he would be ready with examples to back up every fault he had listed for her.

To the husband's dismay, the wife dismissed her own imperfections with a shrug. "What really gets me," she said icily, "is how you could be so blind, so short-sighted, so much of a stuffed-shirt that you would name so few of your own faults. Let me refresh your memory a bit."

While the husband sat chagrined, she proceeded to cite chapter and verse of all his shortcomings. It took almost a week before their relationship was back to normal.

By way of contrast, a minister at our clinic fondly remembers a criticism he received early in his career. One of his first churches was in Syracuse, New York, where the congregation included professors from Syracuse University. "I wanted to make a good impression," the pastor said "So I was constantly thumbing through my dictionary for the right words. As a result, I paid more attention to phrasing than to my message."

The minister had preached several such sermons when one of his good friends at the university dropped in to see him. The friend seemed to have nothing on his mind, so the two men just chatted. The professor related little anecdotes about the congregation, emphasizing always that Syracuse was a wonderful place and that the church was filled with wonderful people.

"You must get to know the young Presbyterian minister," the professor continued. "He makes a deep thought sound so simple." Then he lightly told about another pastor, no longer in Syracuse, who tried so hard to impress university intellectuals that few understood him.

When the professor ended his visit, the young minister made two mental notes: first, he liked the professor very much; second, he would strive for simplicity in the future. Not until later did it occur to him that the professor's seemingly casual visit did have a purpose, which was to give constructive criticism about his own too wordy sermons.

This was criticism applied by a master. Criticism can be positive; undeserved praise can be negative. Jesus knew how to apply criticism gently, yet incisively. His enemies thought they had Him trapped when they brought before Him a woman taken in adultery. The law was that she be stoned. If Christ suggested mercy, He broke the law.

To Jesus, however, the woman's partner in adultery and the hypocrites in the crowd were equally sinful. To them He said, "He that is without sin among you, let him first cast a stone at her." (John 8:7)

He did not embarrass the woman, lying piteously at His feet, by staring at her. When the others had slunk away, knowing in their hearts that they were equally guilty,

Jesus gently bid her go. But not without saying, "And sin no more."

Before plunging ahead with criticism which you mean to be helpful, ask yourself these questions:

Do I have a compliment to give before I start?

Is there a smile on my face—and in my heart?

Am I sure of my facts?

Will our talk be in private?

Have I considered ways of making my point without unnecessary bluntness?

Most important—never criticize anyone until you have prayed for him first.

No matter how well-meaning you are in your criticism, however, you will never get along with people unless you balance your criticism with the fourth word, *praise*. People have starved egos. They crave flowers and compliments while they are alive, not tributes at their funerals.

The young wife of a magazine editor has such a genuine interest in people that she has hundreds of close friends. "I believe in telling people I like them right to their face—if I really do, that is," she said. "I never had many compliments when I was a girl because my parents seemed to feel that if they praised me, it might go to my head. As a result, I felt inferior, unwanted. Because I know from personal experience how starved people are for praise, I speak right out when I like something about someone. And it's surprising how much you can find to like in others if you look for it."

During a social affair this young lady will make a point to speak to everyone present in a personal way. She avoids general compliments such as "You look very nice," but, instead, singles out some one special item for comment. It might be an attractive hair-do, a gay hat, a pretty scarf, a unique brooch, or a beautiful dress. In many cases, she happens to select for attention a prized possession. As a result, people greatly love this young woman.

A survey taken among industrial workers revealed the surprising information that most employees are more interested in commendations and credit for work done than in pension plans or improved working conditions. The boss who is free with words of praise will find they can do magic.

Four methods for getting along better with people are the proper use of love, politeness, criticism and praise. A fifth involves *thoughtfulness* of others, a way of getting rid of self-consciousness. Obviously one who thinks of self constantly hasn't the time or capacity to endear himself to someone else.

A young man approached a minister at our clinic in confidence one day. "Whenever I go into a room full of people, they all keep staring at me. Everything I do sounds wrong. I freeze up."

"What makes you think everyone is looking at you?" the minister asked.

The boy thought for a moment. "I don't know exactly. But I feel their eyes on me."

"Do you do something to attract their attention when you enter the room?"

"No. On the contrary, I try to slip in without anyone seeing me."

Patiently, the minister tried to make the boy see that people were not always looking at him. He had built up this self-reference habit in his own mind to the point where he imagined it all. He was thinking of himself, dwelling on how he walked, how he looked, and how he talked, rather than on what others were doing and saying.

The psychiatrist also worked with the boy, trying to help him understand the reason for his self-consciousness, which in this case resulted from a too dominating father and a mother who had been too protective.

It was suggested that the boy follow a specific procedure whenever he was in a social group. The key word he was to keep in mind was Thoughtfulness. First, he was to look about the group for the shyest, most neglected person there, and give this person special attention, inquiring about his or her interests. He was to help this person to get away from a feeling of self-consciousness.

Second, he was to look for things to compliment, both in people and around the house.

Third, he was to remember that people will like you if you can raise their spirits. Too many are depressed and discouraged. Bring cheerfulness into a room, and people will want to know you and be with you. So he was asked to say this prayer, "Lord, fill me with joy, let the radiance of Christ saturate my mind and reveal itself through me. Let this joy run through my whole physical being and transmit itself to others. Let me have love for life; fill me with love for people." He was to repeat this prayer over and over.

"There will be times when this process will seem very difficult," the minister told the boy. "When this happens, hold this thought, 'If God be for us, who can be against us?' (Romans 8:31) He will help you say the right thing, tell you how to do the right thing. As He helps you, your confidence will develop, your shyness will disappear and you will begin to act with naturalness."

Deeply involved cases of self-consciousness, as this boy possessed, are not resolved quickly. A long period of treatment was needed before the young man began to relax and develop a naturalness with people.

So these are five key words for success in your relationship to others: Love, Politeness, Criticism, Praise and Thoughtfulness. If you are to master these arts, though, you will certainly want to fortify yourself with a few special techniques for coping, not only with the ordinary person, but also with the difficult person. Every office has one person in this category. So does your social club; so do most churches; you meet this difficult person in every walk of life.

What is he like? In the office he is the person who has a sharp comment for everything: the weather, the coffee, his wife, his neighbors, the people on the bus, his cleaner, the movie he saw last night. He tops it off by finding fault with the worker who sits next to him.

In his club he criticizes the way finances are handled, the social program, the people who are running the activities. In his church, he feels that the young people are hopelessly wild, and says so vehemently. The minister isn't preaching on the right subjects, that church members are hypocrites, and so on.

Garry Moore of television fame recently told a story that points up an effective counter-weapon against the bitterness of such a person. The story was about a Chinese restauranteur named Wong. For years Wong struggled along with a small establishment, in downtown Los Angeles, saving everything he could in the hope of moving his restaurant to one of the suburbs. When the time came, Wong happened to choose a location near the Garry Moore home. It was a good location. There was only one other Chinese restaurant nearby, a highly successful, long-established place run by a man named Ling Toy.

Garry first learned about the battle that was shaping up between the two men when he went, one night, to Ling Toy's restaurant.

"Have you heard the news, Mr. Moore? The city has licensed a fool to open a restaurant across the street."

All through the meal, Garry was barraged with invectives aimed at the newcomer. "He has cockroaches in his kitchen . . . He doesn't know the art of Chinese food blending . . . He is going around telling everyone untrue stories about me and my restaurant. You won't listen, when he collars you, will you Mr. Moore?"

Actually, Ling Toy so berated his competitor that it spoiled Garry's dinner. The next time the Moores went out to eat, they decided to try Wong's restaurant more to escape Ling Toy than for any other reason. They found the restaurant clean and the food delicious. Once during the dinner they overheard a customer telling Wong about some of the stories Ling Toy was passing around. Wong's reaction was immediate and firm.

"I'm sure there must be some mistake," Wong said. "You must have misunderstood. Ling Toy couldn't have said such things. He's too genuinely kind."

Still Ling Toy's campaign continued. He accused Wong of every breach of good faith imaginable, and each time Wong returned the slander with a compliment. No man can stand against an attack of kindness for long, and gradually Ling Toy's ranting slipped off until suddenly one morning, as if nothing had ever been wrong between them, he walked into Wong's restaurant, stuck out his hand and said:

"I've been meaning to come over for a long time. Welcome to the neighborhood. I hope we will both succeed."

Hearing this, Garry Moore visited Wong and complimented him on the way he had handled the whole affair. Wong smiled. "It is not my wisdom," he said, leading Garry out to the kitchen. "I took my cue from this old Chinese saying." He pointed to a sign hanging over the kitchen door, where Wong saw it every time he walked out into his restaurant. The sign said simply:

The enemy is best defeated who is defeated with kindness.

If you have a problem with a difficult person, here are some additional techniques to follow:

First, if a blow-up occurs between you and this other person, give yourself a few minutes to cool down. Then do something which may seem difficult, even ridiculous. *Give thanks for this personality problem.* There is a great therapeutic value in thanking God for a difficulty, because it changes thought patterns from resentment and bitterness to the idea that, "Here's an opportunity for me to learn something."

Second, *express regret as soon as possible,* regardless of whether you are right or wrong. The fact that you show to the other person that you are sorry, even while you feel it wasn't your fault, often produces a startling change for good in the whole relationship. By removing the irritant within yourself, you can break down the hostility of the other person.

Third, no matter how bad the relationship, or how severe the clash or disagreement, close your eyes and imagine (*i.e.* create a mental image) that you and this other person are on friendly, congenial terms again. Visualize, through prayer, the two of you sitting down together laughing and talking easily. Picture all the misunderstandings and disagreements as washed away completely. In this way you are not only asking God to heal the breach between you two, but *you are also visualizing the prayer as already being answered.*

Fourth, *do something immediately, if possible, for the other person.* A small favor or even a compliment about this person to a third party will help. The moment you are angry is the time for a swift act of generosity. Even more effective, sometimes, is to make it possible for the other person to do something nice for you.

You are not being "soft" or impractical when you try this procedure—it takes a great deal of courage and force of character to go through with it all. Try these steps sincerely and honestly, and you will be amazed at how the most difficult situations can miraculously straighten themselves out.

These foregoing techniques were, in effect, the very practical methodology Christ used so effectively in His dealings with others. Nothing better than this has ever been discovered as a means for getting along well with people.

ABOUT THE AUTHOR

NORMAN VINCENT PEALE was born in Bowersville, Ohio, and studied at Ohio Wesleyan University and at Syracuse University. He is the minister at Marble Collegiate Church in New York City. Dr. Peale is the author of one of the most popular non-fiction books of recent times—*THE POWER OF POSITIVE THINKING,* which has been translated into thirty-three languages. With psychiatrist Smiley Blanton, he is co-founder of the Institutes of Religion and Health.

INSPIRATIONAL BESTSELLERS

by Norman Vincent Peale